Reading and Interpreting the Works of

EMILY DICKINSON

Reading and Interpreting the Works of

Lit Crit Guides

EMILY DICKINSON

Enslow Publishing
101 W. 23rd Street
Suite 240
New York, NY 10011
USA

enslow.com

Audrey Borus

Published in 2016 by Enslow Publishing, LLC
101 W. 23rd Street, Suite 240, New York, NY 10011

Library of Congress Cataloging-in-Publication Data
Borus, Audrey.
Reading and interpreting the works of Emily Dickinson / Audrey Borus.
    pages cm. — (Lit crit guides)
Includes bibliographical references and index.
Summary: "Describes the life and works of poet Emily Dickinson"— Provided by publisher.
ISBN 978-0-7660-7344-9
1. Dickinson, Emily, 1830-1886—Juvenile literature. 2. Dickinson, Emily, 1830-1886—Criticism
and interpretation. 3. Women poets, American—Biography—Juvenile literature. I. Title.
PS1541.Z5B554 2016
811'.4—dc23
[B]
                          2015029184

Printed in the United States of America

To Our Readers: We have done our best to make sure all website addresses in this book were active and appropriate when we went to press. However, the author and the publisher have no control over and assume no liability for the material available on those websites or on any websites they may link to. Any comments or suggestions can be sent by e-mail to customerservice@enslow.com.

Portions of this book originally appeared in the book *A Student's Guide to Emily Dickinson.*

CONTENTS

Emily Dickinson

A Poet Like No Other: An Introduction to Emily Dickinson

If you're a high school student or interested in American poetry, you have probably heard the name Emily Dickinson. In fact, some sources say that no poet has ever captivated the reading public's imagination as has Dickinson.[1] You have probably heard that she rarely left home and at a certain point did not go out at all, that she only wore white and that she never wanted the fame she has posthumously achieved. But what do you really know about Dickinson and her poetry? This book will help you sort what is known about her life from the uniqueness of her writing.

Beginnings

It was a very cold December day in Amherst, Massachusetts, a Friday. Emily Norcross Dickinson was going to have her second child. She was probably a bit nervous. Her mother and sister could not come from their home in Monson (a town little more than fifteen miles from Amherst) and she was not on very good terms with her husband's mother or sisters. She had no close women friends in or around Amherst. Because of her status as the wife of Edward Dickinson (a prominent lawyer), she would not use a midwife, who might offer emotional support and let nature run its course. Rather, her new baby was to be delivered by Dr. Isaac Cutler, an experienced doctor who had brought her first child, William Austin, into the world.

Still, Dr. Cutler's specialty was not delivering babies, and most men who practiced medicine (by and large, doctors at that time were men) viewed pregnancy as a form of sickness. Mrs. Dickinson knew that women often died in childbirth and that in her family in particular there were rumors about sickly infants.[2] Then there was Mr. Stebbins. He was painting Mrs. Dickinson's bedroom that very day. She had wanted to have it done earlier, but her husband would not allow it. Nevertheless, she had secretly asked the paper hanger to come, and he was just finishing as she was in labor.[3] It was into this household that Emily Elizabeth Dickinson was born on December 10, 1830, at 5:00 in the morning.

1830s America

Of course, the world was very different in 1830. Railroads were beginning to crisscross the country, connecting places that were formerly unreachable. (Until that time, people had thought of train travel the way we think of travel to other planets.) Canals, like the Erie Canal, had been completed, thus providing water routes from the East Coast to the middle of the country. What this did for the economy and the lives of people is astounding. Goods from the South, such as cotton, could be shipped to the North. And people in Amherst and the Northeast were gradually able to connect with people elsewhere in the developing nation. Still, in 1830, Amherst was fairly agrarian, meaning that most people were farmers and the economy was based on agriculture.

The Dickinsons, however, were a family of scholars and lawyers. Emily's grandfather, Samuel Fowler Dickinson,

The Dickinson family home on Main Street in Amherst, Massachusetts. It was known as the Homestead.

founded Amherst College, which is still a prominent school today. Samuel Dickinson was known to be pious, religious, and a hard and steady worker. Because of the Puritan heritage of the northeastern part of this country, such values were highly regarded. Emily's father, Edward, was the treasurer of Amherst for thirty-seven years. He was also a lifelong trustee of Amherst Academy and very involved in local affairs such as town meetings and the First Church Parish Committee. So, although the Dickinson family was not wealthy, they were well-known.

Children in the 1830s

In nineteenth century America, children were supposed to be seen and not heard. At a very early age, girls amused themselves quietly indoors with their dolls and sewing. Most of the books children read were printed in England during the 1700s and then reprinted in America over and over. Usually, these books had themes from the Bible or were stories about the importance of being hardworking, honest, and obedient. Emily probably learned to read from such books. There were also a few fairy tales she would have known, many of which are still told today, such as *Hansel and Gretel, Rapunzel,* and *Cinderella.*

Before Emily was born, only certain sports were acceptable and then only for boys, who played after school and on weekends. These included activities such as hunting, fishing, boating, and swimming. By 1830 educators were considering the merits of sports for providing moral guidance. Parents started sending their children to private instructors after school to learn "refined" sports, such as light gymnastics and marching as a class. By about 1860, many sports were advocated as healthy, useful, and pleasurable physical activities for young boys. The need for physical activity for girls was also suggested, but sports for girls were not strongly advocated by educators of the day.

At Home With the Dickinsons

When Emily was born, the family lived on Main Street in a large brick house called the Homestead. It was said to be the first brick house in Amherst. Three years later, her sister Lavinia was born, completing the family. There were always dogs, and Emily was fond of one in particular, Carlo. When Emily was nine, the family moved around the corner to North Pleasant Street. Twelve years later, the family moved back to their original home on Main Street, and it was there Emily lived for the rest of her life.

Though nineteenth century Amherst was very different, kids back then felt about their parents as many do today. In a letter to a friend, Emily's brother Austin wrote that father and mother had gone away for an overnight trip: "Emily and I are left lord and lady of the mansion with none to molest or make us afraid. We are anticipating a fine time in the absence of the ancient people. Wish you were here to help make us laugh."[4]

The family remained close, and when Austin married Susan Gilbert in 1856, Emily was overjoyed (Susan and Emily had met at school). Emily's father built a home for the couple next to his own, called The Evergreens.

A Grim Reality

Death was more commonplace in the days of Dickinson's youth. A simple sore throat might have lethal consequences, and many a Sunday sermon dealt with mortality and resurrection. At thirteen, Dickinson had been at her classmate Sophia Holland's deathbed. Even though the doctor ordered her to

Young Emily (left) with her brother, Austin, and sister, Lavinia.

leave when her friend became delirious, Dickinson stayed on because she wrote "It seemed to me that I should die too if I could not be permitted to watch over her . . ."[5] In the house on Pleasant Street, Death was also a neighbor since the village cemetery ran along one side of it. From a north-facing window, Emily could watch funeral processions enter the cemetery's main gate. Some scholars speculate that Dickinson's fascination in writing about loss and fatality may have stemmed from the years she spent living on Pleasant Street.

Emily's Education

Considering that most people viewed education for women and especially adolescent girls as unnecessary, sending Emily to school was a very progressive move. But Edward Dickinson's chief concern for all three of his children (in addition to their health and their duty to be pleasant and obedient) was their education. In this, he echoed his own father's lifelong dedication as well as the

> **idealist poet**
>
> Poets like Emerson, subscribing to the theory that "matter is a phenomenon, not a substance" because it lets them know "the distinction between soul and world" (From "Nature," by Ralph Waldo Emerson).

atmosphere of the town in which he and his family lived. Even before the college was founded, Amherst had a large number of scholars, such as Noah Webster (famous compiler of the first printed dictionary of "American" English in 1828) and Lucius Boltwood, another of Amherst College's founding fathers and brother-in-law to Ralph Waldo Emerson, the famous idealist poet.

The first school that Edward urged all his children to attend was a two-story building of whitewashed brick on the same street as their house. Next, Emily attended Amherst Academy down the street. Classes were as academically demanding as some colleges are today, but Emily was an outstanding student. "We have a very fine school," she wrote proudly to her friend Abiah Root. "There are Mental Philosophy, Geology, Latin, and Botany. How large they sound, don't they?"[6] In many ways, she was a typical teenager. She liked some teachers better than others and gossiped about who was dating whom.

In September 1847, Emily entered the Mount Holyoke Female Seminary in South Hadley, Massachusetts, ten miles south of Amherst. The Seminary founded by Mary Lyon in 1837 was innovative for its approach to women's education: There were rigorous academic entrance requirements, a demanding curriculum, and, conspicuously, no classes in homemaking, though each student had domestic duties. These girls were to be real scholars.

But the school was also quite strict. Every fifteen minutes, bells rang to announce the next activity. The students were expected to obey some seventy rules regarding conduct, health, protection of the building, safety, and contact with the outside world. For example, they had to whisper in halls and work rooms, sleep with doors slightly open, and sit in assigned seats at every activity. Miss Lyon believed strongly in religion, and students were required to attend church services, chapel talks, prayer meetings, and Bible study groups. Twice a day teachers and students spent time in private devotions.

Though she was excited by the prospect of the new school, it took Emily a while to get used to being away, as can be seen in this letter to her brother:

South Hadley, 21 October 1847

My dear Brother. Austin. I can't tell you now how much good your visit did me. My cough is almost gone & my

Emily began attending Mount Holyoke Seminary in 1847, when she was sixteen years old.

spirits have wonderfully lightened since then. I had a great mind to be homesick after you went home, but I concluded not to, & therefore gave up all homesick feelings. Was not that a wise determination? How have you all been at home since last week? I suppose nothing of serious importance has occurred, or I should have heard of it, before this time. I received a loving letter from Mary Warner, last evening & if you see her, please give my love to her & tell her I will answer it the first moment, I have to spare from school.[7]

And then there was the question of religious faith. At the time Emily was growing up, religious revivals were common in New England. Amherst and surrounding towns clung to Puritan beliefs even as other towns such as Boston began to experience great social changes and radically new and different ways of thinking about God and society. For example, Unitarians in Boston were a strong presence in the Massachusetts Legislature and vocally opposed traditional Puritan education. Perhaps because Edward Dickinson traveled back and forth between villages and large metropolitan areas, and the family read several newspapers and all journals like the *Atlantic Monthly* (whose editor, Thomas Wentworth Higginson, would figure greatly in Dickinson's writing life), Emily may have been exposed to some of these ideas. It was hard for her to accept the religious underpinnings of Mount Holyoke. Writing to Abiah about another friend, she gives us a glimmer of her doubt:

> I presume you have heard from Abby, and know what she now believes—she makes a sweet, girl Christian, religion makes her face quite different, calmer, but full of radiance, holy, yet very joyful. She talks of herself quite freely, seems to love Lord Christ most dearly, and to wonder, and be bewildered, at the life she has always led. It all looks black, and distant, and God, and Heaven are near, she is certainly very much changed.
>
> She has told you about things here, how the "still small voice" is calling, and how the people are listening, and believing, and truly obeying—how the place is very solemn, and sacred, and the bad ones slink away, and are sorrowful—not at their wicked lives—but at this strange time, great change. I am one of the lingering bad ones, and so do I slink away, and pause, and ponder, and ponder, and pause, and do work without knowing why—not surely for this brief world, and more sure it is not for Heaven—and I ask what this message means

MOUNT HOLYOKE

Mount Holyoke College exists today and is still an all-women's college, though you probably won't find students whispering in the halls anymore. About 2,200 students from all over the United States and eighty countries around the world attend the college. It was the first school in the cluster of women's colleges known as the "Seven Sisters," a name that comes from the Pleiades star cluster (a constellation containing seven stars). The distinguished colleges that make up the academic constellation are: Barnard, Bryn Mawr, Radcliffe, Smith, Vassar, Wellesley, and, of course, Mount Holyoke. The "Seven Sisters" nickname was adopted in 1927, when the schools organized to promote private, independent women's colleges and "separate but equal" liberal arts education for women. Until that time, most colleges and universities were open to men only.

that they ask for so very eagerly, you know of this depth,
and fulness, will you try to tell me about it?[8]

In spite of the fact that Edward Dickinson believed in educating his daughters, he was not without biases. He did not think much of most of the popular writers of the day such as Harriet Beecher Stowe and Emerson. His ideas were rooted in nineteenth century Puritan New England; he believed in moderation, hard work, the power of reason over passion, and the virtue of self-denial. Novels, he thought, were frivolous. In an 1862 letter, Dickinson wrote of her father:

I have a Brother and Sister—My Mother does not care for thought—and Father, too busy with his Briefs—to notice what we do—He buys me many Books—but begs me not to read them—because he fears they joggle the mind.[9]

And what few professional women there were, Edward did not hold in high regard. While engaged to Emily's mother, Mr. Dickinson wrote a series of articles for an Amherst newspaper under the pseudonym of "Coelebs." He claimed that women, while they should be educated, had their duties to perform— namely: childrearing, cooking, and cleaning. Imagine the problem for Emily, challenging her father's conventional and religious viewpoints. Her questioning nature would contribute to the strength of her poetry.

Eventually Emily came home without finishing Mount Holyoke. There were probably a number of reasons for this, such as poor health and her rebellion against the religiousness and strictness of the seminary. Her father may have wanted her home, or perhaps she never got used to being away.

Everything and the Kitchen Sink

In nineteenth-century America, housework was very hard and people hired servants (or domestics) to undertake these chores. Since matches had not been invented, servants maintained the fires used for heating and cooking. Just to keep a house running, servants had to cut and haul wood, sweep and haul ashes, and clean up the soot when poorly vented chimneys smoked in a downdraft. There were candles to make or smoky lamps to fill and trim.

Kitchen chores included open-fire cooking and maneuvering iron cranes, spits, and heavy cast-iron pots. Utensils turned black with soot. To gauge the temperature of an oven, the cook had to hold her hand inside the heated oven and count the number of seconds she could tolerate the pain. Just think how hot the kitchen would be in summer! Until refrigeration was introduced in about 1834, meat spoiled in a day, and poultry could not be killed more than four hours before it was cooked. Milk soured in half that time. Water was hand-carried, often from inside the house to a washing house outside, so doing laundry was a long and tiring task.

Emily's mother spent time cooking and caring for sick relatives and friends in addition to managing her own busy household. Even with the help of Emily and Lavinia and a woman named Mrs. Mack hired to help with the laundry, Mrs. Dickinson still had a lot of housework.

Following their mother's lead, the Dickinson sisters baked for neighbors and, in their own home, developed the habit of splitting the work during periods when they did not have additional help or their mother was ill. Cleaning fell most often to Lavinia, while Emily was cook and baker. Dickinson was not

The hallway outside Dickinson's bedroom at the Homestead. She and her sister, neither of whom ever married, lived in the house for almost all of their lives.

fond of the work. She once wrote, "I don't keep the Moth part of the House—I keep the Butterfly part."[10]

To add to the daily workload, the Dickinsons entertained a great many guests. As a prominent family in town, they were very involved with its society. And as part of Amherst College, Edward Dickinson and his wife were well known for their commencement receptions. There was a "steady stream of visitors, many of them famous or near-famous, who enjoyed their hospitality."[11]

Throughout her life, Dickinson wrote about the housework she did. Sometimes she complained that her parents "regulated" and "settled" her and her sister Vinnie with housework (letter 182). In the 1840s she describes herself as doing "everything," mentioning the piles of mending that awaited her return after a month away with relatives (letters 5, 9, 14). In the early 1850s, many of the poet's letters to friends addressed how hard she had to work. She complained to friend Jane Humphrey in 1850, "Vinnie away—and my two hands but two—not four, or five as they ought to be—and so many wants—and me so very handy—and my time of so little account—and my writing so very needless" (letter 30). In one of her more plaintive letters written to her friend Abiah, Emily complained of having to choose between doing household chores and accepting an invitation to go for a ride in the woods with a friend:

> While I washed the dishes at noon in that little 'sink-room' or our's, I heard a well-known rap, and a friend I love *so* dearly came and asked me to ride in the woods, the sweet-still words, and I wanted to exceedingly—I told him I could not go, and he said he was disappointed—he wanted me very much—then the tears came into my eyes, tho' I tried to choke them back, and he said I *could*, and *should* go, and it seemed to me unjust.[13]

CLASS DISTINCTIONS

The Dickinsons were part of the middle class, well-off enough to hire domestics to work in their houses and gardens. Many of the people hired to do household jobs were Irish immigrants who were not always treated well and often were not seen as equals. In fact, "behavior" books for young upper- and middle-class women included instructions about how to treat servants. These behavior books also stressed the need to create segregation between the classes. Emily and her sister Lavinia would have been familiar with them.

While Emily has been quoted as making derogatory remarks about Irish immigrants,[12] she did not entirely pay attention to the common stereotypes. For example, she chose Tom Kelley (Maggie's brother) as her chief pallbearer, along with five other Irish men who worked the Homestead grounds. For Irish Catholics, the significance of this honor would not go unnoticed, nor would Dickinson be unaware of it.

Really, how many of us would hang around doing house-work? And yet she did. In a sense, it wasn't really a choice for her—the expectation was that she would help—but how must that have felt?

The Help

In 1850 Lavinia and Emily, then teenagers, convinced their father to hire help. While it was customary in places like Boston and New York for women of their class to have servants, in Amherst the girls were expected to help their mother. Edward Dickinson placed an ad in local paper looking for a "girl or woman who is capable of doing entire work of a small family."[14]

The family appears to have had a number of Irish immigrants as maids before hiring Maggie Maher. It is interesting to note that people of the Dickinsons' social standing found the Irish to be alien because of their religion and language; the Irish were often ridiculed and worse.[15] Ironically, Maher was only expecting to stay with the Dickinsons for a few months before joining her sister and brother-in-law in California. She ended up staying for thirty years, becoming much more than a maid or a cook to the family. Says one Dickinson scholar, "Emily and Maggie formed a relationship that was at once unfair and close."[16] It was Maggie who undertook a lot of the extra housework so that Emily could write. Many Dickinson scholars also believe that Maggie knew about Emily's writing and later protected at least some of it from being burned.

Choosing Friends

Though Emily Dickinson always seemed to have friends, it doesn't seem she liked people very much. When asked about her companions, Dickinson replied "Hills—and Sundown—

Josiah Holland began working as an editor at the *Springfield Daily Republican* in 1850. He and his wife Elizabeth became close friends with Dickinson.

and a Dog—large as myself, that my Father bought me—They are better than Beings—because they know—but do not tell."[17]

So who did Emily Dickinson choose for friends? Josiah Holland, an editor at the *Springfield Daily Republican*, for one. Emily knew him and his wife Elizabeth, and they came to call at The Evergreens. Only a few years older than Emily, Elizabeth became a favorite of the poet and Lavinia. The sisters visited the Hollands in Springfield and throughout the poet's life Mrs. Holland remained Emily's closest female friend outside the family.

stanza

A grouping of the verse-lines in a poem, often set off by a space in the printed text.

While at Amherst Academy, Emily had been a very lively and sociable companion. She made many friends, but the two girls she corresponded with most were Abiah Root and Jane Humphrey. Though she wrote them many letters, they do not appear to have captivated her as they got older, and eventually those correspondences stopped.

At Amherst Academy, Emily also met Susan Gilbert, and by 1850 they had become quite close. After Susan married Emily's brother Austin in 1856, Emily wrote her a little poem with this first stanza:

> One Sister I have in our house
> And one, a hedge away.
> There's only one recorded,
> But both belong to me.[18]

Susie was an important person to Emily and probably knew her poetry well. But as time went on, relations between the two became strained. It is possible that Emily felt left out during the early years of Susie and Austin's marriage. The rift most likely grew when Emily (devoted as always to her brother) sided with him after he had an affair with writer and editor Mabel Loomis Todd.

Another of Dickinson's early associations was with Benjamin Franklin Newton of Worcester, Massachusetts. He was a law student in Mr. Dickinson's office late in 1847, and though it is reported he did not attend college, he must have had an intellect and seriousness that Emily's father respected. The men in Edward's office were always welcome at the Dickinson home, so Ben Newton visited there. He introduced the Dickinson girls to the writing of the Brontës and Emerson and is probably one of the few of Emily's earliest friends who was able to recognize her promise as a poet.

Emily may have been possessive about her friendships, and she also seems to have associated friendships with fear and loss. In 1853 Ben Newton died. A few days after he died she wrote a note to her brother: "Oh Austin, Newton is dead. The first of my own friends."[19] He was still on her mind twenty years later when she wrote another correspondent, "My dying Tutor told me that he would like to live till I had been a poet."[20]

My Friends Are My Estate

Emily was almost thirty when she met a remarkable man at her brother's home. He was rather handsome and had a wonderful personality. As editor of the *Daily Republican*, which was owned by his father, he wrote clear and pointed editorials. In fact, he was well on his way to making the paper nationally respected. His name was Samuel Bowles, and he was known for his independent thinking. He was also a bit of a ladies' man, somewhat self-absorbed. But Emily did not care about that as much as finding someone to parry with her. So she began to write him letters; their correspondence would last almost twenty years.

Dickinson wrote the following in a letter to Bowles around 1858:

> My friends are my "estate." Forgive me then the avarice to hoard them! They tell me those were poor early, have different views of gold. I don't know how that is. God is not so wary as we, else he would give us no friends, lest we forget him![21]

There is also evidence that Dickinson once loved a man named Otis Phillips Lord. A graduate of Amherst College, Lord studied law and was admitted to the bar in 1835. Emily was twenty-six when she met him, a married man at the time. They wrote each other often, and when his wife died in 1877, they began to enjoy what Emily's niece called "adventures in conversation."[22] Most of all, he was fun, literate, and intellectual; in short, he understood Dickinson.

Then there are the three letters probably written in 1861 or early 1862, to someone Dickinson referred to as "Master." They are clearly love letters, and scholars have speculated broadly who this master may have been. One likely candidate was Reverend Charles Wadsworth, a Presbyterian pastor Dickinson is thought to have met while visiting a friend in Philadelphia. The other possibility was Samuel Bowles. Both were married men.[23]

There was one other friend who was important to Dickinson in her later life: Colonel Thomas Wentworth Higginson, a radical minister of the Free Church in Worcester, Massachusetts. With Higginson, the poet maintained a friendship from the 1860s until her death. As people did in those days before cell phones and email, the two wrote letters. Dickinson initiated the correspondence in 1862 when

Higginson was a published writer and critic. Most Dickinson scholars think that Emily saw the lead article Higginson had written for a famous literary magazine called *The Atlantic Monthly*. The article, titled "Letter to a Young Contributor," gave practical advice to beginning writers and made a call for submissions. Many Dickinson experts agree that Emily must have read the article and felt encouraged to write him. Whatever compelled her, their correspondence lasted twenty-one years, and though it is said that Higginson did not really understand her verse or publish it during her lifetime, she did choose him to be her critic and often sought his advice on her work. He, for his part, considered Emily's poetry difficult, but he also appeared to think she was worthy of his time and attention.

Helen Hunt Jackson, a poet and novelist who had grown up in Amherst, was one writer who had confidence in Dickinson. The two had lost contact over the years, and Colonel Higginson re-acquainted them. Mabel Loomis Todd also believed in Dickinson's originality and talent. Though she never actually met Dickinson, she later collaborated with Higginson to produce the first published collection of the poet's work.

Times of Change

By the mid-1850s, Amherst was entering a period of significant change. Manufacturing was on the rise. Two of the largest factories in town—the Leonard Hills Company and the Henry D. Ferring Company—made hats and were large enough that the Dickinsons could see both from their windows. All in all, life was good, and the Dickinsons were for the most part a well thought-of, even influential, family.

Author Helen Hunt Jackson would prove to be an important figure in Dickinson's life, encouraging her to keep writing.

But trouble was brewing. Because the country's economy was expanding so rapidly, some people wanted the government to provide protective tariffs (taxes) on imports.

People in the North and the growing western part of the country wanted the federal government to sponsor the building of roads, railroads, and canals. The South, however, had little interest in these projects. As public lands in the West were beginning to be settled, the focus turned toward free farming. Quarrels developed over the high tariffs, which protected the Northern manufacturers. The South wanted a low tariff so it could trade its cotton to Great Britain and other countries for cheap foreign goods. Thus began the Civil War.

Though Amherst was never directly in the line of fire, it was affected. By the time the war was over, the town had lost many of its quaint New England ways, and more and more people were moving from the country into the larger cities, seeking better prospects than farm life could offer. At the same time, immigrants from Europe poured into metropolitan areas all over the country, and despite the enormous casualties on both sides during the Civil War, America's population increased to over thirty-eight million. Then over eleven million additional immigrants arrived and the nation was transformed forever.

Even though Emily Dickinson is often described as reclusive or withdrawn, she was not oblivious to the events going on around her. She read newspapers and journals and would have been aware of all the changes going on in the country. Still, while some of her letters and poems reflect these events, it appears she consciously withdrew and devoted herself to her craft: the art of writing.

> This is my letter to the world,
> That never wrote to me,—
> The simple news that Nature told,

With tender majesty.
Her message is committed
To hands I cannot see;
For love of her, sweet countrymen,
Judge tenderly of me! (#441)

Though recent scholarship has revealed that some of Dickinson's "literary practices" were less unconventional than previously thought,[24] Emily Dickinson did break ground with the breadth of her subject matter, and her reclusive, unconventional lifestyle. Whether seen as the Belle of Amherst or its Virgin Recluse, today nearly all her writings are recognized as American classics. In truth, Emily Dickinson was a poet like no other.

READING POETRY: UNDERSTANDING EMILY DICKINSON'S POEMS

There is more to poetry than just the words themselves. Poems, more so than novels or newspapers, require attention to detail. The way they look (i.e., their form) and the words an author chooses have a heightened value when compared to prose. Poems use what William Shakespeare called "the mind's eye,"[1] meaning that your emotions and experiences help you to understand what a poem means. A good way to approach poetry is to read it slowly and carefully. Try reading a poem aloud and more than once.

With Emily Dickinson's poetry in particular, it's important to keep a few other things in mind:

- Be open to surprise. Dickinson made use of unusual vocabulary, often using the secondary definition of a word, or perhaps making up a meaning. She also used irregular rhyming schemes and dense syntax that sometimes require you to dig deeply for meaning.

- Be open to multiple meanings. Keep in mind that a poem doesn't have one interpretation. Often Dickinson didn't have one meaning, but rather a progression of ideas.

- Be prepared to add a word or two. Dickinson's poems are so compact that it may seem at first that she's left out something. Think about what words that might create meaning and don't be locked into one possibility. Some collections of her poems reveal that she had more than one way of expressing her ideas; sometimes looking at these variations can help you.[2]

Use a Bible concordance. Dickinson knew the Bible well. You may encounter an unfamiliar image or word that is an allusion to a passage from the King James Version. A good concordance for you to use is James Strong's *The Exhaustive Concordance of the Bible*, which is keyed to the one Dickinson knew.

concordance

An alphabetical list of all of the words in a book or in a set of works written by an author.

When you first approach a poem, some things may make sense to you immediately. For example, Dickinson wrote the following poem in about 1868, when she was almost forty years old:

Tell all the Truth but tell it slant—
Success in Circuit lies
Too bright for our infirm Delight
The Truth's superb surprise
As Lightning to the Children eased
With explanation kind
The Truth must dazzle gradually
Or every man be blind—. (#1129)

In this poem, consider the word "circuit." It comes from the word "circle" and can mean an indirect route. One interpretation is that the way to the truth may not be the most direct route ("Tell all the Truth but tell it slant/Success in

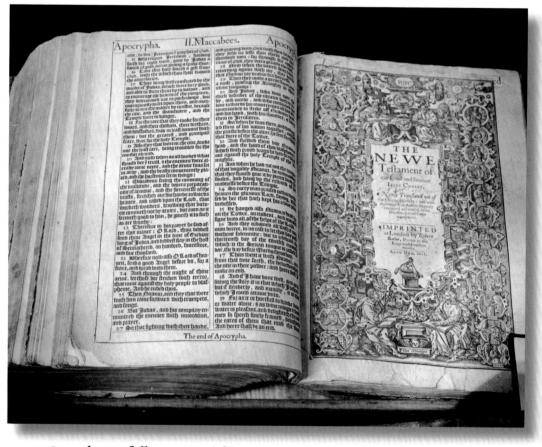

In order to fully grasp Dickinson's poetry, it is helpful to have an understanding of the King James Bible, with which she would have been very familiar.

Circuit lies"). By capitalizing the words "Truth" and "Circuit," Dickinson employs a commonly used poetic device, personification; that is, she makes "Truth" and "Circuit" proper nouns, like people.

Dickinson's Literary Devices and Conventions

Like many poets, Dickinson used an assortment of literary devices: metaphor (comparing two objects with the intent of giving clearer meaning to one of them), simile (comparing two objects using a specific word of comparison such as "like," "as," or "than"), alliteration (the repetition of sounds), personification, and symbolism (a form of metaphor in which a person, place, thing, or quality takes on a more complex meaning).

Punctuation

Dickinson did not use conventional rhyme, capitalization, or punctuation. For example, she put dashes not just at the end of a line, but also within the lines.

Examine this poem:

> The Brain—is wider than the Sky—
> For—put them side by side—
> The one the other will contain
> With ease—and You—beside—.

alliteration

Repetition of initial sounds at the beginnings of two or more words.

allusion

A passing reference, without explicit identification, to a literary or historical person, place, or event, or to another literary work or passage.

Notice that lines one, two, and four all contain interior dashes that help control the poem's rhythm. Emily Dickinson is widely believed to be the first well-known poet to depend on dashes this way. Some believe she used the dash for emphasis, to indicate a missing word or words, or to replace a comma or period. Other readers suggest that the dashes are similar to the punctuation and meter of the sort of hymnal with which Dickinson would have been familiar. Still others point out that common grammar textbooks of the day (such as William Harvey Wells' Grammar of the English Language, which Emily would have used at Mount Holyoke Seminary) condoned using dashes and capitalization to stress and personify common nouns.

---

meter (metre)

A measure of the rhythmic quantity of a poem, the way organized succession of groups of syllables are organized at basically regular intervals in a line of poetry, according to definite metrical patterns. In English this is by accented and unaccented syllables in the words.

---

personification

A metaphor that attributes human characteristics to inanimate objects, animals, or abstract ideas.

Capitalization

Another feature of Dickinson's poetry is unusual capitalization. In many of her poems Dickinson capitalizes common as well as proper nouns.[3] Though she may have derived her use of capitals from German, which she studied at the Amherst Academy, such usage has other effects, one of which is making common things seem more important.

For example, a "spider" becomes a "Spider," as if it possessed a proper name and a personality. In addition, the unusual use of capitalization is eye-catching.

Though in the early twentieth century most poetry was written to be heard, that notion of verse was beginning to change. Starting perhaps as early as Dickinson, the focus began to shift to a poem's visual properties. Some critics think that Dickinson may have even moved that process

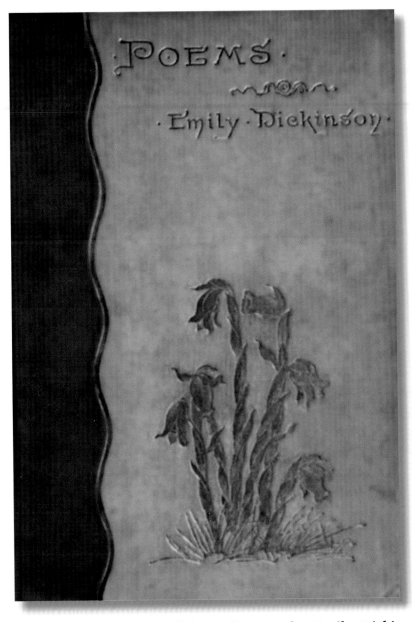

The cover of the first edition of *Poems* by Emily Dickinson, published about four years after her death. Only a handful of Dickinson's poems were actually published in her lifetime, many of them anonymously.

along by rebelling against the conventions of grammar and punctuation.[4]

Meter and Rhyme

rhyme
The repetition of identical or similar sounds in unaccented syllables of words. An "eye" or "sight" rhyme is one in which words are similar in spelling but different in pronunciation, like "mow" and "how" or "height" and "weight." Dickinson frequently used sight rhyme.

rhythm
Recurrence of syllables at regular or expected intervals.

Dickinson used meter, the rhythmical pattern of syllables stressed in lines of verse, in a way not found in most nineteenth century poetry. Many of her poems consist of alternating lines of eight and six syllables with an alternating pattern of unstressed and stressed syllables, known as common meter. Back then such a scheme was used in American nursery rhymes and in hymns.

For example, the following two lines from one of Dickinson's poems (#204) show how this works; the unstressed syllables are marked with a (ˇ) and the stressed syllables are marked with a (/).

ˇ / ˇ / ˇ / ˇ /
Put gently up the evening Bars—
ˇ / ˇ / ˇ /
And led the flock away—

Dickinson also experimented with traditional rhyme schemes, frequently replacing them with partial rhymes or with words that sounded alike but did not quite rhyme. Sometimes she used sight rhymes, sometimes in the form of visual jokes such as words that are spelled as if they rhyme but do not (for example, *word* and *lord*).

DOES THE SOUND FIT THE SENSE?

One measure of good poetry is to ask yourself "Does the sound fit the sense?" Poets write with an ear to the "music" of their words. They use various sound devices to make their verses "sing" so that their work has an enhanced meaning when read aloud. The music in poetry is not always pretty; a poem about a horse may have a short, clipped sound, while a poem about the incoming tide may have a pounding, urgent rhythm.

Before the twentieth century, poetry was generally characterized by certain formal sound and structure devices such as meter. Meter is the pattern of beats and pauses that creates the rhythm of poetic verse. In Emily Dickinson's time, if it did not have meter, it was not poetry. Modern poets have written increasingly in free verse, poetry without a set rhyme scheme or meter. Still, poets writing free verse use many sound devices and may create their music by using alliteration, assonance, and onomatopoeia. Emily Dickinson uses all of these to create a unique voice and to enhance meaning in her poems.

Sometimes Dickinson used no rhymes at all, and while that may not seem so unusual today, it was extraordinary at the time.

Visual and Physical Aspects of Dickinson's Poetry

One may wonder about the layout of Dickinson's poems on a page and how she decided where to break lines. "Your thoughts dont have words every day" she says in one of her poems (#1452), and perhaps this line echoes your own feelings about trying to write. In addressing the challenge of finding just the right word for a thought, Dickinson puzzled over the many ways to place words on the page. We know because she left behind a copy of this poem with a dozen different words and phrases crossed out and placed differently within it.

Another thing to keep in mind is the physical presentation of Dickinson's work. She included poems in letters to her many correspondents, and although she was not the only person to do this (her Aunt Elizabeth once sent Austin a rhymed letter of fifty stanzas about his toothache), she was quite inventive and prolific. Dickinson also wrote on scraps of paper, then bound these together (more than eight hundred poems) into forty booklets (known as fascicles). Her original editors, Mabel Loomis Todd and Thomas Wentworth Higginson, took them apart after her death so we may never know exactly how she intended them to be read.

---

simile

A resemblance or comparison between two generally unlike things, usually introduced by "like" or "as."

---

symbolism

A form of metaphor in which a person, place, thing, or quality stands for a more complex meaning.

Language/Diction

As for all writers, words were Dickinson's tools, but the way she used the words was unusual. While other women authors wrote in a long, flowery style, Emily Dickinson fit her complex ideas into short, tight sentences with vocabulary that most women did not use. Dickinson critic Charles Anderson comments that "in her best writing [she] was never at the mercy of her emotions."[5] Rather, "she mastered her themes by controlling her language."[6] She borrowed the words of many professions, such as law, medicine, and the military, and she took her meter from English hymns. Small wonder that composers like Aaron Copeland have set her poems to music and dancers like Martha Graham wanted to choreograph them.

Dickinson loved language and enjoyed words for their own sake. One of her amusements was reading *Webster's Dictionary* (1844), savoring words and their definitions. A number of her poems take as their form definitions of words—for example, "Success Is Counted Sweetest," "The Bible is an Antique Volume," and "Hope is the Thing with Feathers."

Dickinson liked to change the function or part of speech of a word, using adjectives and verbs as nouns. For example, in "We Talk in Careless—and in Loss," "careless" is

assonance

The repetition of vowel sounds within words or the rhyming of vowels rather than whole words. Rather than selecting two words that rhymed, Dickinson often used assonant rhyme in her poetry so she could make the most apt word choices.

onomatopoeia

A word that imitates the sound it names.

an adjective used as a noun. She frequently uses "be" instead of "is" or "are."

Dickinson's linguistic mastery and sense of the dramatic combine as she creates striking first lines for her poems, such as "The Brain is Wider than the Sky," "I Felt a Funeral in My Brain," and "A Route of Evanescence."

Occasionally, it seems as though Dickinson created private meanings and symbols, using them as if everyone else was in on their meaning. So there are times when her language, instead of communicating, can be baffling. Consulting a nineteenth-century dictionary may also be useful in grasping Dickinson's meaning, at times.

"Who are you?"

In many poems, Dickinson does not identify a particular character. However, this does not mean that a poem does not have one. For example, in "I'm Nobody! Who are you?" the speaker asserts that being a "nobody" is a much better lifestyle than being judged or even observed by an "admiring bog." In this instance, the bog is like a character, perhaps the politicians who were visiting her father constantly or the congregation at church that she no longer attended.

> I'm Nobody! Who are you?
> Are you—Nobody—too?
> Then there's a pair of us!
> Dont tell! they'd advertise—you know!
> How dreary—to be—Somebody!
> How public—like a Frog—
> To tell one's name—the livelong June—
> To an admiring Bog! (#288)

When Dickinson wrote this poem in 1861, she was already becoming a "nobody" herself; she had stopped going

Dickinson's bedroom at the Homestead. Although the poet evidently preferred her own company, she actively maintained written correspondences with friends and acquaintances.

to Sunday church services, retreated to her room when most guests visited the Homestead and entered into a period at which she was her most productive.[11] Dickinson's biographers often mention that she preferred a life of seclusion to a life of admiration. Could the "nobody" to whom Dickinson refers be the person she longed to be?

Common Themes

Dickinson's writing deals with all the stuff of life: nature, love and death, time and eternity. She treated these themes in a manner

43

GORGEOUS "NOTHINGS"

Emily Dickinson collected her poems in fascicles. She drafted the poetry on whatever paper was at hand (even the backs of envelopes), then copied them onto pieces of folded, unlined paper, often striking out words and adding others. She arranged the sheets of paper in a stack, punched two holes on the left side, and bound them together with string, creating packets of sixteen pages containing twenty or more poems. In 1981 Ralph Franklin compiled *The Manuscript Books of Emily Dickinson*, arranging the poems as close to the way Dickinson arranged them as possible. This collection of the fascicles lets us see the poet's unconventional use of punctuation as well as her deliberation over different words. Not surprisingly, the existence of the overlapping versions has made for many interpretations of Dickinson's poetry.

When Dickinson died, 1,775 poems were found bound into fascicles.

Maggie Maher, the Irish maid who worked for the Dickinsons for thirty years, did a lot to protect the fascicles. Apparently Emily stored many of them in Maggie's trunk. As was common practice in the 1800s, Dickinson asked that her correspondence be burned after she died.[7] Since many of her poems were contained in letters, when Lavinia burned them, she burned the poems as well. But according to Dickinson's niece, Martha Dickinson Bianchi, Maggie went to Susan and Austin with the writings stored in her trunk "in an act of disobedience that preserved a literary treasure."[8]

Maggie was also the person responsible for handing over her copy of a daguerreotype you often see reproduced in books on Emily Dickinson. Taken in about 1847 when Emily was seventeen years old, it is the only uncontested photo we have of her today.

In April 2000, Philip F. Gura, a professor of American literature at the University of North Carolina, placed a bid on eBay for a "vintage Emily Dickinson albumen photo." (Albumen, the white of an egg, was used in a common process for developing photographs in the mid-1860s.) Professor Gura won the bid and went about trying to authenticate the picture. It is an exciting story, but not everyone is convinced the photo is authentic. Writes Gura, "I (and many others) continue to believe that the image genuinely is of Dickinson, and my state of mind regarding it was beautifully summed up in an editorial about the image in the (Durham) *Herald-Sun*. . . . 'Although the forensic analysis of Gura's photo strongly suggests the woman is ED, no one can say for sure. By the same token, no one apparently can say that the woman is NOT Dickinson. Thus is Philip Gura caught in neutral buoyancy between belief and hope. Or, maybe that's the way ED wanted.'"[9]

all her own: often with humor and playfulness, but also with seriousness and sensitivity. Many of her poems use the pronoun "I" as their central speaker or *persona*. This "I" seems to speak directly to us, making observations that are at once obvious and indecipherable. As writer Joyce Carol Oates once suggested, what Emily Dickinson questions is "meaning itself."[12]

Dickinson took her writing very seriously and dedicated herself to finding poetry in every aspect of day-to-day life. The themes of life: love, spirituality, or the belief in something outside the physical world, and jealousy and despair, repeat themselves throughout her work. But while Dickinson's insights are profound, some think they are limited in topic. The critic Northrop Frye once commented that he would be hard pressed to name another English-speaking poet with so little interest in social or political events. And though Dickinson lived through the Civil War, until recently scholars thought she wrote little about it. As you will see, the war did surface in Dickinson's poetry, but its presence is not overt.

Accessing Emily Dickinson

"Dickinson's poetry is challenging because it is radical and original in its rejection of most traditional nineteenth-century themes and techniques," explains author Michael Meyer.[13] Read her poems actively, paying attention with all your senses. It may help to read them aloud; what may seem puzzling on "a silent page"[17] can make more sense if you hear it, listening for the pauses around the dashes, the sounds of the words themselves. Also keep in mind that Dickinson, like every human being, was not always consistent in her views; her viewpoint can change from poem to poem. It seems she was less interested in finding answers to questions than in examining their meaning, their "circumference."

ARRANGING THE POEMS

Dickinson was a prolific writer who left behind many, many poems. They were in quite a state: some had been hastily stuffed into Maggie Maher's trunk, Lavinia had burned some, and Dickinson had bound others together with needle and thread into the fascicles. In 1955 a three-volume critical edition edited by Thomas H. Johnson set a new standard for Emily Dickinson students and scholars the world over. His book contained 1,775 poems in chronological order (as far as he could determine). He examined the originals and published them in their first form, leaving out other editors' punctuation marks and titles.

In 1967 another Dickinson scholar, Ralph W. Franklin, revised Johnson's ordering and added some other poems he had found. Mr. Franklin kept working on this project until 1981, when he attempted to fully restore the poet's original arrangement. Guided by such evidence as the imperfections of her stationery, smudge patterns, and puncture marks where Dickinson's needle had pierced the paper to bind them, Franklin returned the poems to their original order. Still more recently, Sharon Cameron argued that the way Emily Dickinson bound her poems had less to do with the order in which she wrote them (the chronology) than with their theme.[10]

Decoding

"There have been, there are now, and there will continue to be contests over not only who owns Emily Dickinson's words but what object can be called a poem by Emily Dickinson. There are many objects that can be called poems of Emily Dickinson, but what constitutes a poem by her has never been firmly established."[18]

Only ten of what most would call Dickinson's poems were published during her lifetime and then only anonymously. Because her style was so unusual and experimental, her original editors (Thomas Wentworth Higginson and Mabel Loomis Todd) tried to conceal it. They thought her peculiar punctuation was an obstacle to reading rather than an integral aspect of her verse, so they "corrected" it, along with her spelling, many of her rhymes, and other unusual features of her poems in manuscript. For this reason, her work appears in different ways, sometimes with inline dashes, sometimes without. In one version a word may appear with initial capitals while in another collection the word will be in lower case.

In addition, Dickinson never gave any of her poems titles; Todd and Higginson did. The two editors also grouped the poems according to principles of their own that did not reflect Dickinson's arrangement. These groupings included Time and Eternity; Life/Love; Nature.

In the following chapters, we will look at Dickinson's better-known works and try to unravel their meaning in a process called explication, which literally means "an unfolding." We will refer to the poems and letters by the number that Thomas H. Johnson, one of the first scholars to organize her work, gave them.

THE ENVELOPES, PLEASE

In 2013, Dickinsonians Marta Werner and Jen Bervin put together a full color edition of Dickinson's later writings, which she wrote on the front and backs of envelopes. Entitled *The Gorgeous Nothings*, the book emphasizes visual aspects of Dickinson's work that have been previously unexplored. For one, these envelope works reflect a lesson made plain in *The Frugal Housewife*, "a book Dickinson's father obtained for her mother when Emily was born."[14] "Preserve the backs of old letters to write upon," the book admonishes. And so Emily does. And as *The Gorgeous Nothings* indicates, Dickinson opened those envelopes quite carefully. As Bervin notes, this tells us as much about Dickinson as it does about her milieu. "Dickinson's envelope writings convey a sense of New England thrift and her relationship to the larger household economy of paper, but they also disclose private spaces within that household: the line "we should respect |the seals of | others —"inscribed next to gummed seal [of one of the envelopes] resounds."[15]

From this volume, we also learn that Dickinson's lap desk is ridged with fine cuts and gouges, consistent with her cutting the envelopes in particular ways. From this, the authors conjecture that she was very much aware of her composition space, in much the same way a visual artist is, and that these works should be considered for not just the words but for their visual aspects as well. Dickinson sent more than three hundred poems to correspondents in her lifetime [16] and was not secretive about the fact she was writing. However Dickinson allowed so few of her poems to be published during her lifetime, we can only guess about her intention.

For Further Study

Several Dickinson poems mentioned earlier are worthy of further study. Note word choice and use of language and see if you can find any additional significance in any of these poems.

Success is counted sweetest
By those who ne'er succeed.
To comprehend a nectar
Requires sorest need.

Not one of all the purple Host

Who took the Flag today
Can tell the definition,
So clear, of Victory

As he, defeated—dying—
On whose forbidden ear
The distant strains of triumph
Burst agonized and clear! (#67)

***

"Hope" is the thing with feathers—
That perches in the soul—
And sings the tune without the words—
And never stops—at all—

And sweetest—in the Gale—is heard—
And sore must be the storm—
That could abash the little bird
That kept so many warm—

I've heard it in the chillest land—
And on the strangest Sea—

Yet, never, in extremity,
It asked a crumb—of Me. (#254)

***

The Bible is an antique Volume—
Written by faded Men

At the suggestion of Holy Spectres—
Subjects—Bethlehem—
Eden—the ancient Homestead—
Satan—the Brigadier—
Judas—the great Defaulter—
David—the Troubadour—
Sin—a distinguished Precipice
Others must resist—
Boys that "believe" are very lonesome—
Other boys are "lost"—
Had but the tale a warbling Teller—
All the Boys would come—
Orpheus' sermon captivated—
It did not condemn— (#1545)

A Funeral in My Brain:
Life, Death, and In Between

Emily Dickinson spent much of her early life in a house whose windows looked out on a cemetery. More than that, children knew that many illnesses could prove fatal. Diphtheria, scarlet fever, and whooping cough were common diseases in the 1800s, and many children died before they reached the age of sixteen from the sorts of things we do not even think about today. Minor cuts and scratches became infected or cures administered by well-meaning parents and doctors turned out to be harmful. Death was common and, being the keen observer she was, Dickinson often wrote about it.

As scholar Joan Kirby notes, at the time Dickinson was writing, notions of death as a purely religious event had begun to change. "Death was cut loose from its theological moorings and people encountered death without the promise of afterlife."[1] There were a variety of interpretations about what happened to one in death: from the idea that the living could communicate with the dead through mediums to how a corpse might decompose. Emily Dickinson would have been aware of these discussions.

In Dickinson's day, many people died young. This woman is suffering from scarlet fever, a common and often fatal malady at the time.

Death

Before the age of technology and medicine, people were more resigned to death. Friends and family often crowded into the dying person's room waiting and watching, as if death were a movie or play. Commonly, people brought gifts, and those who had led less than ideal lives were urged to repent. Those gathered would sing hymns, and finally the dying person might whisper that he or she felt God in the room. Of course, not every death was like this, but such a scene would have been familiar to Emily Dickinson and her family.

> I'll tell you how the Sun rose—
> A Ribbon at a time—
> The Steeples swam in Amethyst—
> The news, like Squirrels, ran—
> The Hills untied their Bonnets—
> The Bobolinks—begun—
> Then I said softly to myself—
> "That must have been the Sun"!
> But how he set—I know not—
> There seemed a purple stile
> That little Yellow boys and girls
> Were climbing all the while—
> Till when they reached the other side—
> A Dominie in Gray—
> Put gently up the evening Bars—
> And led the flock away— (#318)

At first glance, this seems to be a poem about nature and wonders of a sunrise and sunset, the beauty of a day. But as Helen Vendler points out, the day is precisely what's left out.[2] She notes that on the original poem, Dickinson had drawn a horizontal line between the second and third stanzas. Perhaps she intended to write two poems, as one of her early editors,

Ralph W. Franklin suggests. But Vendler sees another explanation. The line Dickinson drew separates the poem into two eight-line stanzas, one for sunrise and the other for sunset.

Describing the gradual sunrise as "ribbons," the poet reflects on how it lights the town steeple, then more quickly spreads "like Squirrels ran," illuminating the Hills and the Bobolinks who chirp awake. "'I'll tell you,' says Dickinson, with absolute confidence in her ability to narrate the birth of the day. Ah—but what of the day? 'But how he set, I know not.'"[3] This change in tone—from certainty to doubt lets us know that Dickinson isn't merely talking about the beginning and end of a day; she's talking about life and death, inexplicable because none of us knows how our lives will end. Dickinson imagines that it might be like a sunset with little Yellow boys and girls repeatedly running over a purple stile 'till they reach the other side where a Dominie (schoolteacher) in Gray helps them across to the evening Bars. Vendler notes that this is an allusion to the Twenty-Third Psalm, with the schoolmaster standing in for Jesus. The children are gathered up never to return.

Consider the images in this poem:

I heard a Fly buzz—when I died—
The Stillness in the Room
Was like the Stillness in the Air—
Between the Heaves of Storm—

The Eyes around—had wrung them dry—
And Breaths were gathering firm
For that last Onset—when the King
Be witnessed—in the Room—

I willed my Keepsakes—Signed away
What portion of me be

Assignable—and then it was
There interposed a Fly—

With Blue—uncertain stumbling Buzz—
Between the light—and me—
And then the Windows failed—and then
I could not see to see— (#465)

Dickinson critic Caroline Rogue suggests that this poem begins with a standard nineteenth-century deathbed scene. From the beginning, Dickinson builds the scene: the stillness of the room, the family members whose "Eyes around—had wrung them dry." But, notes Rogue, at the crucial moment, when the sufferer is about to draw his last breath, "There interposed a fly." And what kind of a fly? A noisy one, a fly "with Blue—uncertain stumbling Buzz."[4]

Why is the fly there? Some critics like the poet John Ciardi have interpreted it as "the last kiss of the world."[5] Others think the fly represents the realities of a Victorian household; flies were as present in death as in life and Dickinson could be saying that death is as commonplace as a fly. And yet there is the odd line, "With Blue—uncertain stumbling Buzz." How can a sound be blue? Perhaps what Dickinson intends to describe is what she thinks it is like to die. Instead of the great here-after, could it be that people just slip from consciousness? That they fail to "see to see?" Charles Anderson and Betsy Erkkila propose that underneath such a supposition lies a tremendous break from the conventional attitudes of the time.[6, 7]

In Chapter 2 we talked about some common poetic tools or devices. Here's a poem in which Dickinson masterfully uses personification:

Because I could not stop for Death—
He kindly stopped for me—

The Carriage held but just Ourselves—
And Immortality.

We slowly drove—He knew no haste
And I had put away
My labor and my leisure too,

For His Civility—

We passed the School, where Children strove
At Recess—in the Ring—
We passed the Fields of Gazing Grain—
We passed the Setting Sun—

Or rather—He passed Us—
The Dews drew quivering and Chill—
For only Gossamer, my Gown—
My Tippet—only Tulle—

We paused before a House that seemed
A Swelling of the Ground—
The Roof was scarcely visible—
The Cornice—in the Ground—

Since then—'tis Centuries—and yet
Feels shorter than the Day
I first surmised the Horses' Heads
Were toward Eternity— (#712)

To begin, this poem presents us with some very vivid images: the setting sun, a horse-drawn carriage, a graveyard ("a House that seemed/A Swelling of the Ground"). By capitalizing "death" and referring to it as "he", Dickinson begins to give the noun the characteristics of a person, perhaps even modeling this "Death" on someone she knew. Death rides in a

CHARLES DARWIN

Charles Darwin was an English naturalist who challenged contemporary beliefs about the creation of life on earth. In his famous work, *On the Origin of Species*, he gave evidence that life was not created by some divine overseer and that it did not go on forever. Darwin's theory of natural selection suggested that no one species is superior to another or is guaranteed persistence over time. Darwin also introduced the idea of randomness as the driving force behind the variety of types in the natural world. In short, he believed that those that best adapted to the changing environment would survive.

His idea of evolution did more than contradict the Bible; it raised the idea that most things in the world had a scientific explanation. As part of his theory, Darwin also proposed a method for doing scientific research. This was disturbing to nineteenth century society. Although some could reconcile the facts of evolution with their religious beliefs, many others had their faith shaken. Many could not accept the debate over evolution, or the heartlessness of the eat-or-be-eaten scenario of the natural world. Emily Dickinson, however, appears to have questioned the existence of God endlessly, searching for new symbols to believe in. Poem #216 is an example of that mind set.

Charles Darwin presented ideas that contradicted the commonly held view that the world was divinely created. His theories would have added to the religious doubts that Dickinson already had.

carriage with "I," and it's a special ride, for the carriage holds just the two of them. The poem continues:

> We slowly drove—He knew no haste
> And I had put away
> My labor and my leisure too
> For His Civility

The "I" in this poem knows the trip is final. So the "I" and Death drive leisurely, completely at ease. Indeed, Death's graciousness in stopping at a time when "I" was too busy to stop for him is a mark of special politeness. The "I" willingly puts her work away. Again, because this is her last ride, she can give away her spare moments too.[8]

> We passed the School, where Children strove
> At Recess—in the Ring—
> We passed the Fields of Gazing Grain—
> We passed the Setting Sun—
> Or rather—He passed Us—

Conscious that the "I" is leaving the world, Dickinson resists the sentimental and simply presents the scene: the school children, the fields of grain, and the setting sun. Here, she illustrates all there is about life: youth, maturity and age, and the passage of time in the daily rising and setting of the sun. Children will play, the grain must be harvested, and the day will end, just as life eventually ends for all of us. "[A] bsorbed in the Ring" of childhood games, the players at life do not even stop to look up at the passing carriage of death."[9]

Invoking nature's indifference, Dickinson gives "a kind of cold vitality by transferring the stare of the dead traveler's eyes to the 'Gazing Grain.' " Dickinson transfers the sureness of death "to the living corn while the corpse itself passes by on its journey to immortality"[10]—a very clever way of talking about a complex subject, especially considering that this is a time when poetry is written in a specific style, almost like a formula, and certain topics are dealt with in certain ways.

Then we read about the setting sun (a traditional symbol of death), and it is as if we are in the funeral train, passing the village schoolhouse, the fields, finally arriving at the graveyard. As they pass the sun and near the grave, the poem's cadence (rhythmic flow) of sounds begins to slow. Dickinson describes dew that is "quivering and chill." Some critics think that Dickinson is trying to imagine what it must be like to be buried in the cold, dark ground.

Strikingly, Dickinson describes "only Gossamer, My Gown—My Tippet—only Tulle." A tippet is a cape or a shawl. It was also the long black scarf Anglican clergymen wore over their robes during prayer, and at one time the word was used to refer to a hangman's rope. Tulle is a type of stiff fabric used for veils and shrouds.

Again Anderson provides a helpful interpretation. He points out that this is not the description of "conventional burial clothes." Rather, it sounds like a bridal gown "but of a very special sort."

> **Naturalist movement**
>
> A theory in literature that emphasized scientific observation of life without idealizing it or avoiding the ugly. Compare with Transcendentalism.

Could Death be like a proud father taking his daughter to the altar? If so, the house they pause before ("We paused before a House that seemed/A swelling of the Ground") must be a grave, distinguished by the fact that its roof is "scarcely visible." "The Cornice—in the Ground" must be the trim on the coffin already in the soil.

But the true ingenuity here is the poet's ability to look beyond the physical boundaries of the world. There is something else in the carriage and in the poem besides Death and the speaker, something that exists outside time and location. That something is "Immortality."

Compare the previous poem, written in 1862, with this one written in 1858:

> I never lost as much but twice,
> And that was in the sod.
> Twice have I stood a beggar
> Before the door of God!
>
> Angels—twice descending
> Reimbursed my store—
> Burglar! Banker—Father!
> I am poor once more! (#49)

Here, the exactness of the rhymes gives a sharp and final feeling. The first two lines tell us that Dickinson has lost not one, but two people she cares about. Like a beggar, she feels empty without them as she enters the church. Though she believes they are in heaven, she seems to be calling out to a God who can take many forms and is many things to many people ("Burglar! Banker—Father!"). Still, it's not enough to call out to God: She is feeling her loss, saddened by her friends' absence. Around this time she lost Ben Newton and another friend, Leonard Humphrey.

imagery

The written description of a mind-picture appealing to the reader's senses.

The Afterlife

Closely related to Dickinson's poems about death are those dealing with time and eternity. There is no doubt that Emily was influenced by the religious traditions of the time. God was supposed to be everywhere and be all-knowing. Sometimes her poetry reflects a fear and even anger at this God. Yet there are times when she seems to embrace traditional religious imagery and faith. Many of her poems suggest limits about what a person can know, giving us the idea that she believed in something more powerful than a single human being. At the same time, Dickinson expresses admiration for nature and the human mind.

Here's an example:

Safe in their Alabaster Chambers—
Untouched by Morning
And untouched by Noon—
Sleep the meek members of the Resurrection—
Rafter of satin,
And Roof of stone.
Light laughs the breeze
In her Castle above them—
Babbles the Bee in a stolid Ear,
Pipe the Sweet Birds in ignorant cadence—
Ah, what sagacity perished here! (#216)

According to scholar Alfred Habbeger,[11] when Emily sent the poem next door to her sister-in-law and Susan did not like the second stanza, Dickinson drafted another:

Grand go the Years—in the Crescent—above them—

Worlds scoop their Arcs—
And Firmaments—row—
Diadems—drop and Doges—surrender
Soundless as dots on a Disc of snow

There is a push and pull in this poem, "*stasis* (or steady state) and motion."[12] Most critics acknowledge that on one level the poem is about religion. Good Christians ("Meek members of the Resurrection") are not so important in the scheme of things. No matter how fancy their tombs, there is no way they will live again.

In the first stanza, Dickinson confers a religious view of death, including the confident belief that there is an afterlife. Here, she copies the language of the Bible and of Protestant hymns, especially in the line "Sleep the meek members of the Resurrection." But in the next stanza she directs our attention to what is going on above ground: the light laughter of the breeze, birds chirping, the "sagacity [that] perished here!" *Sagacity* means "perceptiveness," and here we might even say, "aliveness." Looking at the cold white tombs that lock out the sun, can we really believe there is life after death?

To critic Bernhard Frank, there's far more to this poem. "Within ten lines we are introduced to at least seven levels of imagery: religious, sociopolitical, mercenary [concerned only with money], architectural/geometric, nomadic, sexual and musical."[13] He notes what other critics have noted, namely that Dickinson may be mocking the Bible ("Blessed are the meek for they shall inherit the earth," Matthew 5:5) and saying that yes, in fact, the earth is all the living get; that there is nothing more beyond. Like other readers, he also points out that the word "safe" can have more than one meaning. A safe can be a bank vault, which introduces the notion of things that are valuable. "Everything in the poem seems to say, You are what you own: the dead of stanza 1 are ostentatiously buried in alabaster, their coffins lined with satin, their gravestones in place."[14]

Another way of reading this poem is to understand it as the conflict between religion and science. Written between 1859 and 1861, the poem reflects a time when the Christian world was shaken by the conflict between religion and science. Up until then people had believed in life after death, but with the appearance of new ideas about science, including Charles Darwin's *On the Origin of Species* (published in 1859), people were beginning to question that belief.

David Porter, Professor of English at the University of Massachusetts, Amherst, directs our attention to the sound patterns of the poem. He says the push-pull tension in it comes from the rhyme scheme, "for in the opening stanza which describes the tomb where resurrection is as yet unachieved, the rhyme is only approximate."[15] He goes on to show that the second stanza rhymes perfectly and that this gives it a sense of finality.

Bernhard Frank also notices the poet's use of capitals and consonants. "The opening *s* sound establishes the key note of the poem, taken up again in "Satin" and "Stone": It is the sound of silence."[16] That *s* disappears for a while, only to return in stanza 2, next to the "plosive dental" *d* in "Diadems," "drops," "Doges" (dukes) and "dots." Moving between *d*s and *s*s, Dickinson takes us from the vibrancy of life to the silence of death.

At first glance Poem #216 seems simple. Each stanza is self-contained and presents a separate thought about death: the peaceful last sleep of those who have faith; their separateness from the living; the possibility of eternity; the poet as above the ground, looking down, then up into the starry heavens. But as you can see, there is more than one interpretation. This multidimensional nature is one of the things that makes Dickinson's poetry so enduring and widely read.

Another poem we should consider in this chapter is #341, "After great pain."

> After great pain, a formal feeling comes—
> The Nerves sit ceremonious, like Tombs—
> The stiff Heart questions was it He, that bore,
> And Yesterday, or Centuries before?

While some may consider Dickinson's preoccupation with death morbid, it was not all that unusual. In addition to people dying of disease more frequently, Dickinson's strong religious upbringing meant that she was constantly being reminded to prepare herself for death.

The Feet, mechanical, go round—
A Wooden way
Of Ground, or Air, or Ought—
Regardless grown,
A Quartz contentment, like a stone

This is the Hour of Lead—
Remembered, if outlived,
As Freezing persons, recollect the Snow—
First—Chill—then Stupor—then the letting go—

From the first line, Dickinson talks about pain. But what kind of pain? It is not physical. "The Nerves sit ceremonious, like Tombs," writes Dickinson, and one reading is that these nerves resemble a group of people after a funeral, sitting stiffly and quietly in a parlor.[17] Perhaps Dickinson wrote the poem at a time when she was "turning inward" and it refers to "a horrifying psychological catastrophe and its aftermath."[18]

It is possible Emily Dickinson suffered from a personality disorder called schizotypy.[19] People with the disease shy away from face-to-face interaction, withdraw from social events, and act in ways that seem odd. They may, for example, dress or use words strangely. There does seem to be an odd pairing of words in this poem. Notice the images in the lines of the first stanza: nerves sitting ceremoniously, a heart stiff with grief. The feet walk mechanically, "go round / A Wooden way" unable to stay straight.

With this imagery, Dickinson conveys a sense of numbness, a quality of deadness underscored by those feet mechanically moving "regardless" of where they go. The lines seem to hang together, not only by the constant images of stillness and heaviness, but also by the fact that the poet runs down a list of body parts—nerves, heart, feet—that appear to have shut down as the result of grief.

Examine the third and fourth lines of the first stanza ("The stiff Heart questions was it He, that bore / And Yesterday, or Centuries before?") more closely. Who is "He?" Could Dickinson be referring to a divine being, perhaps God or Jesus? If you think of the Heart as a person stiff with pain, not knowing time or place, and the "He" as Jesus, could it be that the Heart, in its confusion, is asking whether Christ bore the cross? This sudden question appears in the poem as if blurted out in a moment of suffering; it's like the Heart is asking "Am I experiencing Jesus's pain?" And because it has lost sense of time, it asks, "Did the crucifixion take place yesterday or centuries earlier?"

Behind such inquiries lies Dickinson's notion that pain is a constant part of human existence. Dickinson asks us to consider that the suffering of one heart is similar to the suffering Jesus must have felt on the cross. This may not seem like an extraordinary notion today, but in 1862 it was very radical.

Further on we read the line "A quartz contentment like a stone." Critics Robert Penn Warren and Cleanth Brooks offer two commentaries on this comparison. "The name of the stone helps to particularize the figure and prevent the effect of a cliché. Moreover, quartz is a very hard stone. And, for one who knows that quartz is a crystal, a 'quartz contentment' is a contentment crystallized, as it were, out of the pain."[20] The second is ironic and rather remarkable. The poet refers to contentment, but this is not the kind of satisfaction we usually think of when we're happy. Rather, this contentment is hard and occurs because of the inability to respond any longer.

The poet has created a scene of lifelessness. In the last stanza Dickinson introduces a new metaphor: freezing persons recollecting snow. "Remembered if outlived," she writes as if to say that the experience of grief is like a death by freezing. First, there is the chill, then unconsciousness (the "stupor") as the body becomes numb, then the last stage in which the body finally gives up the fight against the cold, relaxes, and dies. By mentioning the stages of death by freezing near the mention of the shock of deep grief, the passage becomes a powerful statement about life, death, sorrow, and possibly mental illness.

There is another reason this last metaphor is so moving. The imagery of the first two stanzas describes the "stupor." But the last line of the poem carries a new twist, one that provides a context for all its other imagery. The formality, the stiffness, the numbness of the first two stanzas is all accounted for: By attempting to hold on, and fighting against letting go, this mind is defending itself against grief.

DICKINSON AND RELIGION

The religiousness of the world Dickinson inhabited cannot be underestimated. Angela Sorby writes that Dickinson's formal education reflected the Calvinist beliefs of her community.[21] (Calvinism is a form of Christianity based on the teachings of John Calvin. It stresses the moral weakness of humans in the face of a supreme God. It also supports the doctrine of predestination.) The reason Calvinists supported education is because being able to read and write meant that one could be saved. By careful study, children "steer their inherently evil natures toward redemption."[22]

Matters of Life and Death

Another poem that explores the theme of death begins "I felt a Funeral in my Brain."

> I felt a Funeral in my Brain,
> And Mourners to and fro
> Kept treading—treading—till it seemed
> That Sense was breaking through
>
> And when they all were seated,
> A Service, like a Drum—
> Kept beating—beating—till I thought
> My mind was going numb—
>
> And then I heard them lift a Box
> And creak across my Soul
> With those same Boots of Lead again,
> The Space—began to toll
>
> As all the Heavens were a Bell,
> And Being, but an Ear,
> And I, and Silence, some strange Race
> Wrecked, solitary, here—
>
> And then a Plank in Reason, broke,
> And I dropped down and down—
> And hit a World at every plunge,
> And Finished knowing—then— (#280)

But in this poem, Dickinson seems to be describing something beyond death, what Helen Vendler calls "an account of a mental breakdown [that] obliterates consciousness.[23] First, the structure of the poem: parallel clauses strung together by the conjunction "and," repetition of the words "treading" and "beating," and "breaking."

The narrator describes a pain, a "funeral" in the brain that is so intense (it seemed/That Sense was breaking through) it is physical, though the word "Sense" would suggest that Dickinson is referring to a mental space. The Mourners are treading and intrusive, the way thoughts might intrude on someone struggling with a mental breakdown. Then just when it seems the troublesome thoughts may stop, a service begins banging on and on, threatening the narrator until she is afraid she will become "numb" (i.e., lose all sense of reason). Even when the service stops, there's no respite. This time, "Boots of Lead" so frighten the narrator she imagines her coffin and pallbearers.

And then the narrator is outside the coffin, becoming an Ear that hears bells in Heaven, replicating in a way the dissociative state of someone with mental illness. In the end, we must wonder if death is preferable to madness.

For Further Study

Emily Dickinson wrote many poems related to the subject of death and mortality. To follow are several more such poems one might wish to consider for further study.

> A Death-Blow is a life-blow to some
> Who, till they died, did not alive become;
> Who, had they lived, had died, but when
> They died, vitality begun. (#816)

> ***

> Death is a dialogue between
> The spirit and the dust.
> "Dissolve," says Death. The Spirit, "Sir,
> I have another trust."

Death doubts it, argues from the ground.
The Spirit turns away,
Just laying off, for evidence,
An overcoat of clay. (#976)

***

Death is like the insect
Menacing the tree,
Competent to kill it,
But decoyed may be.

Bait it with the balsam,
Seek it with the knife,
Baffle, if it cost you
Everything in life.

Then, if it have burrowed
Out of reach of skill—
Ring the tree and leave it,
'Tis the vermin's will. (#1716)

***

For Death—or rather
For the things 'twill buy,
These put away
Life's opportunity.

The Things that Death will buy
Are Room,—Escape
From Circumstances,
And a Name.

With Gifts of Life
How Death's Gifts will compare,

We know not—
For the rates stop Here. (#382)

***

Death sets a Thing significant
The Eye had hurried by,
Except a perished Creature
Entreat us tenderly

To ponder little Workmanships
In Crayon or in Wool,
With "This was last Her fingers did,"
Industrious until—

The Thimble weighed too heavy,
The stitches stopped—themselves,
And then 'twas put among the Dust
Upon the Closet shelves—

A Book I have—a friend gave—
Whose Pencil—here and there—
Had notched the place that pleased Him—
At Rest—His fingers are—
Now—when I read—I read not—
For interrupting Tears—
Obliterate the Etchings
Too Costly for Repairs. (#360)

DIVINEST SENSE: TRUTH, FAITH, AND REALITY IN DICKINSON

By all accounts, although Emily Dickinson became a recluse in her mid-thirties, she was a keen observer. She knew she saw things differently from the majority of those around her. In 1861 she wrote a letter to her cousins Frances and Louise Norcross with this observation: "Think Emily lost her wits—but she found 'em likely. Don't part with wits long at a time in this neighborhood." (L234).

Lea Bertain Vozar Newman asks us to consider why Dickinson refers to herself in the third person, a literary device that introduces uncertainty: *Who* thinks Emily is crazy? Without a noun or pronoun to go with the verb "think" we don't know if the speaker is an "I" or a "They."[1]

And what about the word "likely?" Does it mean she only might have recovered from a mental lapse and is still rather imbalanced? Or could it be that she was never unbalanced in the first place and didn't need to recover at all? Or, given the observation "Don't part with wits long at a time in this neighborhood," it could mean that she has just been acting "normal" to conform to everyone's idea of how she should behave.

Two years later, Dickinson would write this poem:

> Much Madness is divinest Sense—
> To a discerning Eye—
> Much Sense—the starkest Madness—
> 'Tis the Majority
> In this, as All, prevail—
> Assent—and you are sane—
> Demur—you're straightway dangerous—
> And handled with a Chain— (#435)

The tone and theme of this poem and Dickinson's letter are similar: The "Majority"/"neighborhood" determines what is "normal," and to be left alone, one must "Assent." Recall that in the 1800s, especially in towns like Amherst, social customs were more rigidly defined. Since most people knew each other, most were expected to stop and chat on the street, and probably everyone knew each other's business. Could Dickinson be railing against this etiquette because it is too confining? Dickinson points out that what may be perceived as madness may really be the most sensible course of action, while what's taken for sanity may be quite crazy ("Much Sense—the Starkest Madness").

Ironically, if you "assent," that is, give in, you're considered sane by the "Majority." And when you do not play by the rules and "demur," you're considered an outcast, maybe even "dangerous," and you must be handled with caution. In essence what the poet seems to say is that madness is highly individual; what is right for one person may not be right for another. By taking the time to look with "discerning eye" one learns what is important to him or her.

While on one level the poem is about deception and reality, on another it is about itself.[2] Look at the first three lines of the poem. Biographer Cynthia Wolff explains, "The second line, an adverbial phrase, is what grammarians would call a

A view of the rear of the Homestead, as it appears today. Dickinson understood that her "recluse" lifestyle was considered strange by many people, and addressed the issue in her poems and letters.

'squinting' modifier."[3] That is, it modifies what comes before it as well as what comes after. To make sense of the first and third lines, which by themselves seem contradictory, you need the middle line. Which one is true? Dickinson might quite literally be saying the answer lies between the lines.

Consider again "Tell all the Truth but tell it slant" (#1129):

> Tell all the Truth but tell it slant—
> Success in Circuit lies
> Too bright for our infirm Delight
> The Truth's superb surprise
> As Lightning to the Children eased
> With explanation kind
> The Truth must dazzle gradually
> Or every man be blind—

In this poem, Dickinson appears to be saying that most truth cannot be captured completely in mere words. It is "too bright" for us to accurately perceive. Real truth (particularly divine or religious truth) is too big, too great, and can only be revealed to us a little at a time—otherwise we would be struck "blind" by it.

Another variation of this interpretation is that Dickinson may be saying that revealing too much may not always be wise. At times, Dickinson demonstrated such a philosophy in her own everyday life. For example, when Dickinson first began corresponding with Colonel Higginson, she told him about her feelings of loneliness and terror, about her family and her love life, of her turning to nature in her despair: "They [animals and plants] are better than Beings—because they know—but do not tell" (Letter #261, April 25, 1862). But she also withheld her age, the names of her teachers, and the number of poems she had written.

Poem #1129 repeats and amplifies this theme.[4] Dickinson does not so much develop the theme as reword it. Even though there is no punctuation save dashes, the poem contains four complete sentences (line 1, line 2, lines 3–4, and lines 5–8,). Each is really a variation of the first.

Here is another poem illustrating Dickinson's power of observation and her power as a poet—"I dwell in Possibility" (#657):

> I dwell in Possibility—
> A fairer House than Prose—
> More numerous of Windows—
> Superior—for Doors—
>
> Of Chambers as the Cedars—
> Impregnable of Eye—
> And for an Everlasting Roof
> The Gambrels of the Sky—
>
> Of Visitors—the fairest—
> For Occupation—This—
> The spreading wide of narrow Hands
> To gather Paradise—

The speaker lives in a place called "Possibility," a house whose rooms ("chambers") are "as the Cedars," its roof "the Gambrels of the Sky." "Ah," one may say, "so this is a poem about nature." But this place possesses qualities of something beyond Prose. "This house is Possibility, the imagination. Dwelling there, the lady of the manor makes not cakes but poetry."[5]

Indeed, the house constructed here is one of poetry, its front comparable to a real house.[6] "Dickinson committed herself to the power of poetic vision, which was "More

WHAT IS THE MEANING OF "CIRCUIT" IN POEM 1129?

Dickinson uses the word "Circuit" in the second line of Poem 1129. Today the word tends to be associated with electronics, but its first meaning is "a usually circular line encompassing an area or the space enclosed within such a line."[7] Dickinson has cleverly taken a slanted line ("Tell all the Truth but tell it slant") and curved it ("Success in Circuit lies") in just the way one might "bend the truth."[8]

But when you pronounce the word with stress on the second syllable, "circuit" becomes cir-CU-it, suggesting "circuitous," which means "round-about." (The line might also include one of her sight jokes: "lies" can mean "rests" or "tells an untruth.") By using two words with double meaning, Dickinson underscores her point: If you are going to tell the truth, make sure not to be too sudden or too direct or you might give someone an unwanted surprise or, worse, get an unwanted reaction. (On the other hand, be careful not to go too far, or you may end up telling a lie!)

Another interpretation is that Dickinson may be suggesting that everyone could use a little perspective. "We're always trying to make ourselves look good because we all need to respect ourselves, but if you come at things from an angle, you can often get at some surprises, see more of what's happening in the self and in the world."[9]

Still another interpretation is that this poem may be part of a "constellation," or larger group, of poems in which Dickinson speaks her mind.[10]

Numerous of Windows— / Superior for Doors." This alternative world of possibility was also "Impregnable of eye." It allowed her to "think independently beyond the withering scrutiny of a judgmental society."[11]

A common theme throughout Dickinson's poetry is the power of the imagination to liberate one from public and personal restraints, power to "transform the self" and "gather Paradise."

"The Soul selects her own Society" (#303) turns traditional ideas about power and control upside down:

> The Soul selects her own Society—
> Then—shuts the Door—
> To her divine Majority—
> Present no more—
>
> Unmoved—she notes the Chariots—pausing—
> At her low Gate—
> Unmoved—an Emperor be kneeling
> Upon her Mat—
>
> I've known her—from an ample nation—
> Choose One—
> Then—close the Valves of her attention—
> Like Stone—

In the opening stanza, Dickinson claims that controlling people does not constitute power, but the ability to construct a world for oneself (the Soul) *is* a god-like achievement. Dickinson says the soul is "divine," challenging our ideas about what is sacred. Here again she uses the metaphor of a house to construct an enclosure for the soul. It is a dwelling more adequate for a queenly life than all the chariots or emperors in the world could bring.

The Republican.

ORIGINAL POETRY.

The Sleeping.

Safe in their alabaster chambers,
Untouched by morning,
And untouched by noon,
Sleep the meek members of the Resurrection,
Rafter of satin, and roof of stone.

Light laughs the breeze
In her castle above them,
Babbles the bee in a stolid ear,
Pipe the sweet birds in ignorant cadences:
Ah! what sagacity perished here!
Pelham Hill, June, 1861.

"The Shadow of Thy Wing."

Weary of life's great mart, its dust and din,
Faint with its toiling, suffering with its sin,
In childlike faith my heart to Thee I bring,
For refuge in "the shadow of thy wing."

Like a worn bird of passage, left behind
Wounded, and sinking, by its faithless kind,
With flight unsteady, seeking needed rest,
I come for shelter to Thy faithful breast.

Like a proud ship, dismantled by the gale,
Her banners lost and rifted every sail,
In the deep waters to Thy love I cling,
And hasten to the refuge of Thy wing.

O Thou, thy people's comforter alway,
Their light in darkness, and their guide by day,
Their anchor 'mid the storm, their hope in calm,
Their joy in pain, their fortress in alarm!

We are all weak, Thy strength we humbly crave;
We are all lost, and Thou alone canst save;
A weary world, to Thy dear arm we cling,
And hope for all a refuge "'neath Thy wing."

Did Dickinson refuse to have her poems published while she was alive? Scholars still debate that question today. She did share her work with family and friends, and some of her poems that appeared in newspapers may have been submitted without her consent. These two poems appeared in the *Daily Republican* in 1862.

Even as the speaker claims "divine Majority" and thus her equality with those most powerful in the "real" world, she declares her difference from them. She uses the vocabulary of everyday life: door, low gate, and mat, to point out that her dwelling is not a grand palace but a simple house. Although Dickinson associates power with the enclosed space of the mind, her poem suggests that too much seclusion may not be good. When the soul turns in upon her own concerns, she closes "the Valves of her attention— / Like Stone—."

Helen Vendler's interpretation of this poem focuses on its structure and word meanings. She notes how the 4-2-4-2 rhyming scheme "catches us up short at the end of every two lines, in a long pause as a door is shut."[12] The Soul of this poem chooses its Society (friendships) from an ample nation, then closes the door. Furthermore, Vendler thinks that Dickinson uses the word "valve" to mean what Webster defined in 1844 as "a membranous partition within the cavity of a vessel that opens to allow the passage of fluid in one direction and shuts to prevent its regurgitation." She says that the verb "shut" links the definition to the poem and that knowing that word "valve" comes from *valvae*, the Latin for "folding doors," takes us right back to the poem's first stanza. But the definition also could apply to the heart, with its chambers and valves, and the "Valves of her attention" refers to a love interest. Once that love is achieved, the heart closes to anyone else (close the Valves of her attention— /Like Stone—). Just as Dickinson was inspired by pain and loss, she equally rejoiced in nature and creativity. She once wrote Austin:

> You are reading *Arabian Nights*, according to Viny's statement. I hope you have derived much benefit from their perusal & presume your powers of imagining will vastly increase thereby. But I must give you a word of

advice too. Cultivate your other powers in proportion as you allow Imagination to captivate you! Am not I a very wise young lady? (L19)

"I taste a liquor never brewed" (#214) describes the giddiness of creation, comparing it by metaphor to the feeling of being drunk. (Intoxication is a common metaphor for powerful feelings; for example, "he's drunk with love.")

I taste a liquor never brewed—
From Tankards scooped in Pearl—
Not all the Frankfort Berries
Yield such an Alcohol!

Inebriate of air—am I—
And Debauchee of Dew—
Reeling—thro' endless summer days—
From inns of molten Blue—

When "Landlords" turn the drunken Bee
Out of the Foxglove's door—
When Butterflies—renounce their "drams"—
I shall but drink the more!

Till Seraphs swing their snowy Hats—
And Saints—to windows run—
To see the Tippler
Leaning against the—Sun!

Dickinson plays with the intoxication metaphor by developing it literally and concretely. In the 1800s poets like Ralph Waldo Emerson wrote about wine, but here Dickinson refers to beer with "Tankards" and to drink not made from "Frankfort Berries." Her liquor (the beauty of the things around her) is even more precious.

Lisa Melani at Brooklyn College suggests that in stanza two the speaker tells us she is drunk on air and dew (A "debauchee" is someone corrupted or debased, usually by alcohol).[13] The speaker is so intoxicated that she staggers. Drunk with summer's splendor, the sky appears intensely blue or "molten."

Just how long will nature continue to enchant? Melani says stanzas three and four suggest forever. The speaker will "drink in" nature until foxgloves stop blooming and butterflies give up gathering nectar from flowers. She equates nectar and its positive associations with "drams" (a dram is a small amount of liquor), and when she is through with that small bit, she will drink in nature all the more. In expressing her exuberance, the narrator claims that angels will shake their "snowy Hats," and saints will rush to see her. By referring to saints and seraphs (note the alliteration), could Dickinson be suggesting that God approves of this kind of drunkenness?

Just as stanzas three and four run through the day's activities, the sun begins to set, and somehow the speaker is in the sky, leaning against the sun. By using the word "leaning," Dickinson creates a metaphor: the sun as a heavenly lamp-post. There in Heaven and inspired with the joy of life, the narrator can appreciate what the earth has to offer.

Compare this poem to the ones you previously read. Gone are the shadows and references to temperance. Some critics read this poem as Dickinson's confident belief that everyone can be saved and that there are more possibilities than those put forward by the black-and-white religious beliefs of the day.

Still others note that it was one of the few poems published during Dickinson's lifetime. Under the title "The May-Wine," it appeared in the *Springfield Republican* a few weeks after the Civil War began. Critic Betsy Erkkila thinks this may indicate that Dickinson was doing her part to support the sick, wounded, and dying.[14]

Dickinson once wrote to her friend Colonel Higginson, "I find ecstasy in living—the mere sense of living is joy enough" (Letter #342). And clearly, this was a principle she very much cherished. This poem (#249) speaks of such unrestrained love and delight:

> Wild Nights—Wild Nights!
> Were I with thee
> Wild Nights should be
> Our luxury!
>
> Futile—the Winds—
> To a Heart in port—
> Done with the Compass—
> Done with the Chart!
>
> Rowing in Eden—
> Ah, the Sea!
> Might I but moor—Tonight—
> In Thee!

It was certainly not an easy poem to publish, especially in 1891. After Dickinson's death, Colonel Higginson wrote to co-editor Mabel Todd:

One poem only I dread a little to print—that wonderful "Wild Nights,"—lest the malignant read into it more than that virgin recluse ever dreamed of putting there. Has Miss Lavinia [Emily Dickinson's sister] any shrinking about it? You will understand & pardon my solicitude. Yet what a loss to omit it! Indeed it is not to be omitted.[15]

In Colonel Higginson's comments you get a sense of the morality of the time (just the sort of strictures Poem 435 rails

Dickinson's handwritten manuscript of "Wild Nights"

against). As emotional as the poem is, it expresses dreams and desires hypothetically, that is, as if the speaker were guessing at the experience. Dickinson writes: "were I with you" (in other words, "if I were with you") and "might I but," hinting that perhaps the speaker is remembering past pleasures and wishes for more.

The word "luxury" had a different meaning in 1861 than it does today. Then it was used to denote lust and voluptuousness. The phrase "To a Heart in port" is symbolic of a lover's embrace, with the sea as a symbol of passion—just think of the romantic movies you have seen where waves are crashing on the beach. The lovers in this poem give themselves to passion; they have no need for compass or chart, the instruments of control and reason.

Another way to read the poem is to understand it as a religious experience. In this interpretation, the lover is God. Christian mystics (people who are believed to communicate directly with God) often describe the joy they feel while in touch with God as rapturous and full of elation.

For Further Study

The following are some selected poems of Emily Dickinson on the subjects of faith and religion that one may wish to consider for further study.

> God gave a Loaf to every Bird,
> But just a Crumb to Me;
> I dare not eat it, though I starve,—
> My poignant luxury
>
> To own it, touch it, prove the feat
> That made the Pellet mine,—
> Too happy in my Sparrow chance
> For Ampler Coveting.

It might be Famine all around,
I could not miss an Ear,
Such Plenty smiles upon my Board,
My Garner shows so fair.

I wonder how the Rich may feel,—
An Indiaman—an Earl—
I deem that I with but a Crumb
Am Sovereign of them all. (#791)

***

At least—to pray—is left—is left—
O Jesus—in the Air—
I know not which thy chamber is—
I'm knocking —everywhere—

Thou stirrest Earthquake in the South—
And Maelstrom in the Sea—
Say, Jesus Christ of Nazareth—
Hast thou no Arm for Me? (#502)

***

Far from love the Heavenly Father
Leads the Chosen Child;
Oftener through Realm of Briar
Than the Meadow mild,

Oftener by the Claw of Dragon
Than the Hand of Friend,
Guides the Little One predestined
To the Native Land. (1021)

***

For each ecstatic instant
We must an anguish pay
In keen and quivering ratio
To the ecstasy.

For each beloved hour
Sharp pittances of years—
Bitter contested farthings—
And Coffers heaped with Tears. (#125)

WALKING WITH THE DOG: DICKINSON'S NATURAL WORLD

I started Early—Took my Dog—
And visited the Sea—
The Mermaids in the Basement
Came out to look at me—

And Frigates—in the Upper Floor
Extended Hempen Hands
Presuming Me to be a Mouse—
Aground—upon the Sands—

But no Man move Me—till the Tide
Went past my simple Shoe—
And past my Apron—and my Belt
And past my Bodice—too—

And made as He would eat me up—
As wholly as a Dew—
Upon a Dandelion's Sleeve—
And then—I started—too—

And He—He followed—close behind—
I felt His Silver Heel
Upon my ankle—Then My Shoes
Would overflow with Pearl—

Until We met the Solid Town—
No One He seemed to know—
And bowing—with a Mighty look—
At me—the Sea withdrew— (#520)

Emily Dickinson wrote this poem in 1863 and by most accounts, had never really seen the ocean. Scholars have widely varying interpretations: Some believe the images are sexual; others think Dickinson uses the sea to represent death. What is clear, however, is that the poem makes heavy use of symbolism in form of natural imagery: the dew on a dandelion, the hemp-like hands, the tide rolling past a shoe.

The dog is real, and through her letters we know Dickinson walked him and cared for him a great deal. Could the poem be an observation of how nature (the sea) and culture (the town) interact with the dog functioning as the link between them?[1] Or is the poem about the conscious versus unconscious mind (Frigates in the Upper Floor / Mermaids in the Basement)? Could the sea be a sexual predator (The Tide/ Went past my simple Shoe—/And past my Apron—and my Belt/And past my Boddice—too—)? Or could it refer to what some critics call a powerful realization that feelings like love can create emotions too difficult to control? All of these interpretations have been posed, but perhaps Lea Newman summarizes best when she writes that Dickinson wanted first and foremost to be a poet and fought all her life to avoid the distractions, such as sexual fulfillment (which in her day was only available through marriage), that would keep her from that goal.[2]

Of "shunning Men and Women"—they talk of
Hallowed things, aloud—and embarrass my Dog—He
and I dont object to them, if they'll exist their side.
I think Carl[o] would please you—He is dumb, and
brave—I think you would like the Chestnut Tree, I met

91

Nature features prominently in many of Dickinson's poems. A lifelong gardener, she would have had ample opportunity to observe the wildlife, plants, and flowers that could be found in the garden at home.

in my walk. It hit my notice suddenly—and I thought
the Skies were in Blossom.
—Letter to Thomas Wentworth Higginson August 1862

During Emily Dickinson's time, many poets wrote about nature as an inspiration for divine revelation; in other words, the details of the physical word held a lesson about the world beyond. Dickinson's voice, however, was different. Though many of her poems celebrate the marvels of nature, she also writes about its mysterious, even illusory qualities.

In "A Bird came down the Walk" (#328) you get the sense of a bird in motion, hopping down a garden walk, pecking here and there. But this bird is unaware that anyone is watching:

A Bird came down the Walk—
He did not know I saw—
He bit an Angleworm in halves
And ate the fellow, raw,

And then he drank a Dew
From a convenient Grass—
And then hopped sidewise to the Wall
To let a Beetle pass—

He glanced with rapid eyes
That hurried all around—
They looked like frightened Beads, I thought—
He stirred his Velvet Head

Like one in danger, Cautious,
I offered him a Crumb
And he unrolled his feathers
And rowed him softer home—

Than Oars divide the Ocean,
Too silver for a seam—

CARLO

Dickinson was fond of animals, in particular a dog she named Carlo. From her letters and poems, it appears the dog was a Newfoundland or Saint Bernard or some mix of the two and that he lived for over fifteen years. Dickinson scholars think that she named her dog after the dog in Charlotte Brontë's Jane Eyre or the canine protagonist in another popular novel, Reveries of a Bachelor by Donald Grant Mitchell.[3] What is clear is that the dog was large and messy, that he gave slobbery kisses and that petite as she was, Dickinson love her pet. "Though a legend sprang up that Dickinson dressed "wholly in white," she described herself liking "calicoes," and wearing "a brown dress with a cape if possible browner" – a more practical color for a woman covered in dog hair."[4] Maybe the dog lay at her feet while she wrote or slobbered on her writing paper, but when he died, Dickinson quite simply wrote to her friend Thomas Higginson, "Carlo died. Will you instruct me now?"[5] She never had another dog.

Or Butterflies, off Banks of Noon
Leap, plashless as they swim.

As long as the speaker is unseen, nature continues on its spontaneous and informal way, allowing her to continue secretly observing. That she stands apart from the scene is evident: The bird has a worm for dinner and it is raw, an adjective Dickinson sets off with commas for emphasis, while humans cook their food, sticking to meat and potatoes, not worms or other crawling things.

In stanza two, Dickinson further separates the speaker from the scene. As humans we do not consider each drop of dew or blade of grass individually. But this bird can take a thirst-quenching drink from "a Dew." Unconventionally using the article "a" and capitalizing the letter *D*, Dickinson shrinks the entire garden down to bird size, leaving the speaker to tower over it. After washing down his worm, the bird continues his excursion, recognizing his fellow beetle, and stepping aside to let it pass. Still, the bird does not sense its human observer.

In the third stanza, as the speaker stoops to join in, the bird's eyes "hurried all around" and turn into "frightened Beads." The speaker offers a crumb and the game is up; the speaker can no longer remain unnoticed. Both bird and observer find themselves face to face, and the poem's meter, rhyme, and syntax explode. The action in the last six lines is rapid. The bird unrolls his feathers and rolls away faster than "Oars divide the Ocean." With extravagant images, Dickinson renders the speed and distance the bird flies to get home. How different that home is from the human's, as the poet illustrates by using even more fantastic imagery—the silvery ocean, butterflies swimming "off Banks of Noon" and "plash-less as they swim." "Plash" is actually another word for "splash."

"Plashless," however, is a word Dickinson made up—as if to say that all things with wings are of another world.

"A narrow Fellow in the Grass" (#986) begins:

> A narrow Fellow in the Grass
> Occasionally rides—
> You may have met Him—did you not
> His notice sudden is—

Who is this "narrow Fellow in the Grass"? At first, Dickinson makes him move quickly and deceptively; his appearance is "sudden":

> The Grass divides as with a Comb—
> A spotted shaft is seen—
> And then it closes at your feet
> And opens further on—

By passing briefly, this creature divides the grass in one place, then another. But this thing is hard to see and the speaker has been fooled into thinking it may be the lash of a whip. Just as in "Tell all the Truth but tell it slant" and "Much Madness is divinest Sense," the relationship between reality and appearances is deceptive:

> He likes a Boggy Acre
> A Floor too cool for Corn—
> Yet when a Boy, and Barefoot—
> I more than once at Noon
> Have passed, I thought, a Whip lash
> Unbraiding in the Sun
> When stooping to secure it

It wrinkled, and was gone— Dickinson describes the thing in human terms: he's a "fellow" who "rides" and "combs" and who "likes a Boggy Acre / A Floor too cool for Corn." The word "Floor" suggests a house, rather than the outdoors, making the snake even more human.

> Several of Nature's People
> I know, and they know me—
> I feel for them a transport
> Of cordiality—

"Several of nature's people" (creatures like this snake) know and are known by the speaker. She feels "a transport / Of cordiality" for them. Here, "transport" means carried away with emotion and "cordiality" refers to graciousness, or sincerity, suggesting an intimate connection with animals of all sorts. Yet somehow the speaker and the snake remain distinctly different. The last stanza begins with the word "But," almost as a warning, and the speaker feels "a tighter breathing," like you do when you are holding your breath:

> But never met this Fellow
> Attended, or alone
> Without a tighter breathing
> And Zero at the Bone—

If you've ever come suddenly on a snake, you know how startling it can be. Maybe a chill ran down your spine, a "Zero at the Bone." But the word "Zero" also suggests nothingness, an emptiness. On one level the poem is an acute observation of natural life. On another, it hints about dangers that may suddenly reveal themselves. Could Dickinson be using the natural scene to hint that the unknown and perhaps even the fact of death is always with us?

If you think the fractured rhyme and word choice in these poems are an accident, think again. Emily Dickinson did indeed think about these things. In fact, Poem 986 was one of the few printed during the poet's lifetime. It was published in

In her many letters to Thomas Wentworth Higginson, Dickinson wrote about all aspects of her life and writing.

the *Springfield Republican* on February 14, 1866. The editor called it "The Snake" and added punctuation where she did not put it.

Even though the poem was published anonymously, Emily was furious. She wrote to her chosen mentor and friend Mr. Higginson, "Lest you meet my Snake and suppose I deceive it was robbed of me—defeated too of the third line by the punctuation. The third and fourth were one—I had told you I did not print—I feared you might think me ostensible." They had not only added punctuation but altered the way she broke the lines, which is precisely the reason she did not want her work printed ("ostensible" here means "superficial"). If she were upset over a seemingly logical correction, do you think she would not have considered each detail of her work? Furthermore, Dickinson wrote at least two versions of the bird and snake poems. Each copy differs in the way the stanzas are arranged, punctuated, and capitalized. She also changed certain words.

Like many of Dickinson's poems, "There's a certain Slant of light" (#258) uses natural imagery to convey a deeper, more philosophical meaning. Dickinson employs the sunlight on a winter afternoon as an extended metaphor—a metaphor that is drawn out beyond the usual word or phrase by using multiple comparisons between the unlike objects or ideas. In this case, the changing seasons are a concrete symbol of how feelings and emotional states change too:

> There's a certain Slant of light,
> Winter Afternoons—
> That oppresses, like the Heft
> Of Cathedral Tunes—
>
> Heavenly Hurt, it gives us—
> We can find no scar,

WHAT IF?

Poet W.D. Snodgrass got the idea of "de-composing" the poetry of other poets, rewriting them in everyday language. His book De/Compositions: 101 good poems gone wrong, is a collection of his "decompositions."[6] For example, he rewrote "A narrow Fellow in the Grass" like this:

> A Slender creature through the grass
> Occasionally slides;
> You may have seen him but if not,
> Away he swiftly glides.
> The grass divides itself in two;
> You see a spotted form
> And then it closes near to you
> And opens further on.
> He likes a marshy meadow,
> A floor too cool for corn,
> Yet when a child out walking
> I more than once at noon
> Have passed what seemed a whip lash
> Discarded in the sun
> But when I stooped to get it
> It wriggled and was gone.
> Many of nature's creatures
> Are quite well known to me;
> I feel for them a sense of Familiarity
> Yet never met this creature
> Alone or with friends near
> But, frightened, caught my breath
> And felt the grip of fear.

What do you think it does to a poem to have it reconstructed this way? Do you think Snodgrass is serious? Or do you think that perhaps he is asking the reader to consider what makes a poem a poem?

But internal difference,
Where the Meanings, are—

None may teach it—Any—
'Tis the Seal Despair—
An imperial affliction
Sent us of the Air—

When it comes, the Landscape listens—
Shadows—hold their breath—
When it goes, 'tis like the Distance
On the look of Death—

Consider the sounds and Dickinson's word choice: The late afternoon light "oppresses" and causes "despair" and "imperial affliction." It's winter, a time of year when by late afternoon the day is ending. There is the suggestion of death in the "Heft [or weight] / of Cathedral Tunes," and "the Distance / On the look of Death." Could Dickinson be referring to the distance between life and death? The poet further suggests death by the stillness in the lines "When it comes, the Landscape listens / Shadows—hold their breath—."

Most ingeniously, Dickinson takes a property we normally associate with happy occasions (light) and pairs it with the sorrow of death.

For Further Study

To follow are several more selected poems of Dickinson on the subject of nature. Some may seem strictly observational, while others may point toward a deeper meaning.

Nature, the Gentlest Mother,
Impatient of no Child—
The feeblest—or the waywardest,—
Her admonition mild—

In Forest—and the Hill—
By Traveller—is heard—
Restraining Rampant Squirrel—
Or too impetuous Bird—

How fair her Conversation,
A summer afternoon—
Her Household, Her Assembly—
And when the Sun go down—

Her Voice among the Aisles
Incites the timid prayer
Of the minutest Cricket—
The most unworthy Flower—

When all the Children sleep—
She turns as long away
As will suffice to light Her lamps—
Then, bending from the Sky—
With infinite Affection—
And infiniter Care—
Her Golden finger on Her lip—
Wills Silence—Everywhere— (#790)

***

A Prompt—executive Bird is the Jay—
Bold as a Bailiff's hymn—
Brittle and brief in quality—
Warrant in every line—

Sitting a bough like a Brigadier,
Confident and straight—
Much is the mien of him in March
As a Magistrate— (#1177)

***

Nature is what we see—
The Hill—the Afternoon—
Squirrel—Eclipse—the Bumble-bee—
Nay—Nature is Heaven—
Nature is what we hear—
The Bobolink—the Sea—
Thunder—the Cricket—
Nay—Nature is Harmony—
Nature is what we know—
But have no art to say—
So impotent Our Wisdom is
To Her simplicity. (#668)

TESTING THE NATION:
THE CIVIL WAR AND DICKINSON

Many scholars who have approached Emily Dickinson's work have argued that she did not have an interest in politics or the events of the nineteenth century. Rather, they have focused on the structural complexities of her work with emphasis on her family and friends and the themes of nature, love, death, and God. More recently however, Dickinsonians have begun to view Dickinson in the context of her time. Certainly, she was well-read, and well-informed of current events. Her father and grandfather were prominent in Amherst society and politically active. Just because Dickinson did not leave home, there is little reason to believe that she did not let the world in.

Although Emily Dickinson kept to herself, she certainly would have known about the war. After all, Samuel Bowles, the *Springfield Daily Republican*'s editor and publisher, was by then a dear friend. They corresponded regularly, and he and his wife often came to call. They would have brought news to her. Then there was her friendship with Thomas Wentworth Higginson, commander of the first African-American regiment of the Union Army. And there is Dickinson's own correspondence that shows she remained connected to the world even as she chose not to be part of it. One scholar notes, "Of the 1,789 poems in Franklin's variorum edition, over half were written during the years of the Civil War . . . almost 300 were written in 1863, a year of crisis and turning point in the war, when even Union victories such as Gettysburg had become scenes of horrific bloodletting and mass death on both sides."[1]

As Faith Barrett convincingly argues, Dickinson's Civil War poems "test out opposing ideological positions, sometimes skeptically questioning war-time ideologies and sometimes endorsing them." This was possible precisely because Dickinson made the decision not to publish widely and therefore did not have to maintain a consistency in her viewpoint or her aesthetics.[2]

By the summer of 1861, Dickinson wrote Mrs. Bowles, "I shall have no winter this year—on account of the soldiers—

Confederate troops fire on Fort Sumter in 1861, marking the start of the Civil War.

"WAR IS UPON US"

On Tuesday, April 9, 1861, Emily Dickinson's local newspaper, the *Springfield Daily News*, announced: "The conflict deepens in Virginia, and the interest of the country in its decision increases as its state convention approaches a decision." On Wednesday, the paper reported that a portion of a fleet sailing from New York southward had gone to carry supplies to Fort Sumter:

> They say that messengers have been sent to Montgomery and Charleston to inform Jefferson Davis [serving then as Senator from Mississippi, soon to become the President of the Confederate States] of this design, and give them fair notice that if they resist this peaceful movement the responsibility of war will rest upon them.[3]

By Saturday, April 13, the paper declared, "War is upon us." Though the feeling in Washington, DC, was of "great depression in respect to the war news,"[4] life went on in Amherst. There were houses to let, jobs to be filled, and shopping to be done.

Since I cannot weave Blankets, or Boots—I thought—it best to omit the season" (Lt 235). Some people think that this letter shows Dickinson to be sarcastic and unconcerned about the events unfolding, and that she and her family viewed the war as an annoyance, a reality only when it affected the family. For example, when her brother Austin was drafted, he paid the $300 fee to arrange for a substitute. Others think Dickinson felt "especially and personally grieved, for the many young men from Amherst who fought and died."[5] Unlike other poets of the day, such as Walt Whitman, who directly referenced events going on around him, Dickinson's reaction to events is not always obvious. But, as we have learned from reading her work, they are all the more powerful for their indirectness.

> It dont sound so terrible—quite—as it did—
> I run it over—"Dead", Brain, "Dead."
> Put it in Latin—left of my school—
> Seems it dont shriek so—under rule.
>
> Turn it, a little—full in the face
> A Trouble looks bitterest—
> Shift it—just—
> Say "When Tomorrow comes this way –
> I shall have waded down one Day."
>
> I suppose it will interrupt me some
> Till I get accustomed—but then the Tomb
> Like other new Things—shows largest—then—
> And smaller by Habit—
>
> It's shrewder then
> Put the Thought in advance—a Year—
> How like "a fit"—then—
> Murder—wear! (#426)

Dickinson's correspondence with Samuel Bowles, seen here, serves as evidence that the poet was not oblivious to the war raging in the United States, as some critics have alleged.

This poem, probably written in the fall of 1862, coincides with letters Dickinson wrote to her friend Samuel Bowles. A close friend of Austin's named Frazar Stearns had joined the Union Army the previous year and was killed in North Carolina in March of 1862. Emily had written to Bowles: "Austin is chilled—by Frazer's murder—He says—his Brain keeps saying over "Frazer is killed"—"Frazer is killed," just as Father told it—to Him. Two or three words of lead—that dropped so deep, they keep weighing—" (Lt 256). While it's true this poem makes no mention of the war, the speaker repeats the news of death again and again, trying to absorb it just as Austin could not absorb his friend's death. The speaker tries to translate the phrase to Latin, turn it around as if it were an object (Turn it, a little—full in the face), make it "fit" into the present reality, but cannot absorb it. And if it is Frazar to whom Dickinson is referring, the poem is all the more poignant because Dickinson refuses to invoke wartime dogma that families must understand their sons died for a reason. Calling the death, a "Murder," Dickinson makes it clear she has no use for such platitudes.

In another poem written later in 1862, Dickinson seems to change her view.

> Over and over, like a Tune—
> The Recollection plays—
> Drums off the Phantom Battlements
> Cornets of Paradise—
>
> Snatches, from the Baptized Generations—
> Cadences too grand
> But for the Justified Processions
> At the Lord's Right hand (F406, J367)

The Civil War hit close to home for the Dickinson family when Austin's friend Frazar Stearns, pictured here, was killed in battle in 1862.

Written in common ballad form, this poem uses repetition (Over and over like a Tune) to suggest there is comfort in attending to the rituals around death. Unlike "It dont sound so terrible," the focus is not on the death of one solider but an entire army. The tune the speaker hears is too grand to be earthly; rather, it is for the Baptized Generations, the dead soldiers gone to heaven. The dead and living can draw comfort from their faith (Justified Processions) and know that the dead will be "At the Lord's Right hand." Might Dickinson be suggesting in this heavenly scene the battle of good and evil that many saw playing out during the Civil War?

It feels a shame to be Alive—
When Men so brave—are dead—
One envies the Distinguished Dust—
Permitted such a Head—

The Stone that tells defending Whom
This Spartan put away
What little of Him we—possessed
In Pawn for Liberty—

The price is great—Sublimely paid—
Do we deserve—a Thing—
That lives—like Dollars—must be piled
Before we may obtain?

Are we that wait—sufficient worth—
That such Enormous Pearl
As life—dissolved be—for Us—
In Battle's—horrid Bowl?

It may be—a Renown to live—
I think the Men who die—

Those unsustained—Saviors—
Present Divinity— (#444)

One of Dickinson's most respected editors, Ralph W. Franklin, dates this poem to 1863, and in it we can see a blending of Dickinson's two previous viewpoints. Here, the focus is the civilians who have survived and their relationship to the dead. The speaker opens with an honest announcement: It feels wrong to be alive while others are dead. Though the soldiers have died "In Pawn for Liberty—", the speaker questions if the living are worthy ("deserve—a Thing—").

The poem also reckons with the fact that wars cost not only lives but money. It's significant to note that in early 1862 President Lincoln signed the Legal Tender Act, creating the first paper currency for the United States. Well-informed as she was, Emily Dickinson must have known this and in the second stanza likens the printing of dollar bills to the piling up of corpses on the battlefields. But how can we balance the dollars spent and lives lost for Liberty? The speaker suggests that the dead are "unsustained Saviors," or heroes, and though they may have been financially sustained, they were not sustained by "moral or spiritual worth of the civilians whose 'Liberty' they died to save."[6]

Dickinson and Slavery

During the 1850s, the Fugitive Slave Act was a burning topic in Washington. In existence since colonial times, the Act imposed severe penalties on runaway slaves and those who aided them. At first, they applied to white servants as well as black slaves and were continually enforced until slavery was made illegal at the end of the Civil War.

In 1854 one fugitive slave case in Massachusetts thoroughly aroused the public. Anthony Burns, a fugitive slave,

A poster from around 1855 announces a reward for the capture of a runaway slave. The Fugitive Slave Act, which penalized runaway slaves and anyone who tried to help them, became a controversial law in the years running up to the Civil War. Many scholars believe that Dickinson refers to the injustice of slavery in several of her poems.

113

was arrested in Boston on May 24, 1854. The next day, he was taken to court, but lawyers on this behalf were able to postpone the trial for two days. The next evening there was a mass protest meeting at Faneuil Hall in Boston. Thomas W. Higginson, among others, stormed the courthouse where Burns was confined. Although Burns was returned to slavery, it was evident that this sort of ruling would not go over in Massachusetts again. One year later, Dickinson visited Washington (her father was serving a term in the US House of Representatives), where slave laws were still much discussed. She could not have been deaf to such discourse.

Dickinson would not have been unfamiliar with the comparison of the fugitive slaves hunted down by their owners to deer hunted down by hounds: "Thus was I like the hunted deer," wrote the West African slave Olaudah Equiano in his popular 1789 slave narrative. John Greenleaf Whittier's well-known 1850 poem, "A Sabbath Scene," depicts a fugitive slave as she enters a Northern church, pursued by the slave owner:

> Like a scared fawn before the hounds,
> Right up the aisle she glided,
> While close behind her, whip in hand,
> A lank-haired hunter strided.

Now consider "My Life had stood—a Loaded Gun" (#754):

> My Life had stood—a Loaded Gun—
> In Corners—till a Day
> The Owner passed—identified—
> And carried Me away—
>
> And now We roam in Sovereign Woods—
> And now We hunt the Doe—
> And every time I speak for Him—
> The Mountains straight reply—

And do I smile, such cordial light
Upon the Valley glow—
It is as a Vesuvian face
Had let its pleasure through—

And when at Night—Our good Day done—
I guard My Master's Head—
'Tis better than the Eider Duck's
Deep Pillow—to have shared—

To foe of His—I'm deadly foe—
None stir the second time—
On whom I lay a Yellow Eye—
Or an emphatic Thumb—

Though I than He—may longer live
He longer must—than I—
For I have but the power to kill,
Without—the power to die—

There are many interpretations of this poem. Some think it describes male/female relations. Others believe it speaks of Dickinson's rage at the strictures of society that forced her to practice her art privately. But think about the verse in light of the fugitive slave issue.[7] Could the hunted doe be a runaway slave?

Consider this definition of "slave" from the Webster's dictionary that Emily Dickinson would have used: "A person who is held in bondage to another; one who is wholly subject to the will of another; one who has no freedom of action, but whose person and services are wholly under the control of another." If the speaker in Poem 754 is a slave, he or she can speak only for his/her Master. Worse, that slave has no voice or free will, and can be pressed into service helping to hunt

WHAT DO YOU THINK?

Does Poem #77 use slavery as a metaphor? Do you think Dickinson sides with slaves in their need to run away, to keep "a flying attitude?" Seen in this light, the second stanza may be Dickinson's way of responding to Mr. Burns's case in Boston and to many other incidents throughout the North where outraged citizens tried to storm jails of captive fugitives laying in wait for certain return to slavery.

down a fugitive and even carry out a punishment. As a slave, a person is without rights, no "power to die."

Another poem (#77) suggests Dickinson's awareness of the dozens of stories of escaping slaves.[8]

> I never hear the word 'Escape'
> Without a quicker blood!
> A sudden expectation!
> A flying attitude!
>
> I never hear of prisons broad
> By soldiers battered down—
> But I tug childish at my bars—
> Only to fail again!

As early as 1965, critics such as Thomas W. Ford and later in 1984, Shira Wolosky suggested Dickinson made mention of the Civil War in her poetry. However, most experts on Dickinson thought that she "turned inward to pursue no cause but her own,"[9] so interpretations of her work in this light are relatively new. One recently noticed addition to that possible collection of poems is "A Slash of Blue!"

A slash of Blue!
A sweep of Gray—
Some scarlet patches on the way—
Compose an evening sky—
A little Purple slipped between—
Some Ruby Trowsers hurried on—
A Wave of Gold—A Bank of Day—
This just makes out the morning sky! (#204)

According to Lawrence Berkove, there was some contro-versy over dating this poem, but most experts now believe it to be written in 1861.[10] This is significant, Berkove says, because dating it any earlier caused many to overlook it and consider it only on the surface. And on the surface, the poem appears to be just like a painting: a beautiful description of the sky in the morning and again at night. According to Berkove, there are reasons to believe Emily Dickinson wrote it when Bull Run, the first major Civil War battle, was fought.

In Line 5 Berkove notes the reference to "Ruby Trowsers." Union men, of course, wore blue. But one unit, the Zouaves, was modeled after a unit in the French army of the same name. They intentionally dressed in bright colors to signify their high spirits and bravery. And although they were popular, their bold tactics and bright colors made them prime targets, and their regiments often sustained heavy casualties. Berkove thinks that this poem is a metaphor for the war. "'A slash of Blue!' suggests sword thrusts in an attack either by or on Union troops.

The second clause's use of gray suggests the Confederates (and incidentally supplies additional evidence for assuming a later date of composition to the poem, a date after the war had begun). The verb "sweep" can ambiguously refer to either a crowd of Confederates or, alternatively, a victorious attack by

RALLY ROUND THE FLAG BOYS.
VICTORY AT LAST.

A member of the Union Army 5th New York Volunteer Regiment, also known as the Zouaves. Some theorize that Dickinson uses the imagery of the group's bright red uniform in her poetry.

them. "Some scarlet patches on the way" may refer to Zouave troops on the move or, more probably, to battle wounds. The third line establishes the battle as being in progress at evening, but the tranquil verb "compose" suggests a cessation for the night."[11]

There is a lot of color in this poem—scarlet, purple, ruby, and gold—all shades the Zouaves dressed in, and Berkove thinks this coupled with Dickinson's mention of "Some Ruby Trowsers—hurried on" is clear indication that what she is referring to is the war, perhaps even to wounds on the soldiers themselves or the holes created by the casualties of advancing soldiers. "[A] Bank of Day" may be her way of describing how it looks to see many cannons all firing at once to the approaching line ("bank") of troops. "Read mourning" for "morning," says Berkove, "and the last line of the poem sums up the aftermath of battle."[12]

"The Lamp burns sure—within" (#233) is another poem we can read with an eye towards Dickinson's feelings about war:[13]

> The Lamp burns sure—within—
> Tho' Serfs—supply the Oil—
> It matters not the busy Wick—
> At her phosphoric toil!
>
> The Slave—forgets—to fill—
> The Lamp—burns golden—on—
> Unconscious that the oil is out—
> As that the Slave—is gone.

Here, Dickinson refers plainly to a "Slave." This slave provides labor and fuel to guarantee the "Lamp burns sure." The Lamp symbolizes the states of the South, so busy with their day-to-day business that they ignore what their prosperity is built on: slave labor. But a nation that depends so heavily and unthinkingly on its slaves may some day find the slave "forgets" to fill the lamp. And though for a while, it "burns golden on," prosperity may suddenly go out "as that the Slave is gone." How prophetic an image. How fitting for the institution of slavery itself to become a fugitive and for the country to learn it could no longer depend on its own light coming from those who served it invisibly.

For Further Study

To follow are two more poems of Dickinson that may reference war in general, or the Civil War, specifically. In some instances, war references may be intended to represent another idea entirely. Read through each poem and consider what possible messages may lie beneath each one.

> Bless God, he went as soldiers,
> His musket on his breast—
> Grant, God, he charge the bravest
> Of all the martial blest!
>
> Please God, might I behold him
> In epauletted white—
> I should not fear the foe then—
> I should not fear the fight! (#147)

***

> To fight aloud is very brave,
> But gallanter, I know,
> Who charge within the bosom,
> The Cavalry of Woe—
>
> Who win, and nations do not see—
> Who fall—and none observe—

Whose dying eyes no country
Regards with patriot love—

We trust, in plumed procession,
For such the Angels go—
Rank after Rank, with even feet—

And Uniforms of Snow. (#126)

LETTER TO THE WORLD: THE LEGACY OF EMILY DICKINSON

Emily Dickinson is alive and well, and Tweeting. Obviously not, but there is a handle with her name that tweets excerpts from her vast collection of poems and letters. She has over eight thousand followers. Dickinson would have probably liked the notion of social media. She would have been able to reach many people without actually meeting them in person or officially "publishing" her work, because for a recluse, Emily Dickinson was quite communicative. It's estimated that she wrote ten thousand letters during her lifetime.[1] As a poet and thinking woman, Emily Dickinson read a great deal. She wrote extensively to Thomas Wentworth Higginson and many suspect he influenced her tastes. Dickinson took her art seriously and was highly intelligent—probably more so than many of her readers and, later, her editors. She took great care writing poems and letters; often Dickinson made several drafts of her work. When she died, her sister found hundreds of scraps of paper—grocery lists, torn corners of envelops—with her writing.

Dickinson's Literary Tastes

Besides Longfellow, other popular writers at this time included Nathaniel Hawthorne and Ralph Waldo Emerson. Emerson

Emily Dickinson is buried in the same cemetery that her room overlooked when she was growing up. Her gravestone states that she was "called back" on May 15, 1886. The last known letter that Dickinson wrote contained only those two words.

was a famous idealist poet. Dickinson had kept a copy of Emerson's 1847 book *Poems* since her friend and mentor Ben Newton gave it to her when she was twenty. There was Harriet Beecher Stowe, best known for her work *Uncle Tom's Cabin*, and Helen Hunt Jackson, who was also from Amherst. Mrs. Jackson was quite popular in her day, outspoken and widely published. Her insights about Emily Dickinson's poetry reveal more understanding and depth than many other literary figures who judged it, and it is said she had a lot to do with encouraging Dickinson to continue her writing.

Aside from Jackson, the few women writers popular in Dickinson's time followed the convention of flowery words and predictable plots. Though Dickinson liked Emerson, she is said to have been disapproving of poet Walt Whitman—as were many because they found him too risqué—and may have never read him. She is said to have liked the Brontës, especially Emily Bronte's poem "Last Lines." Above all, there was Shakespeare, about whom Dickinson is said to have commented, "Why is any other book needed?"[2]

Though she is often compared to Edgar Allen Poe, Emily Dickinson does not seem to have had as narrow a vision of what a poet should write about (Poe felt that beauty, rather than truth, was most important to good poetry).

Dickinson's Influence

Of course, Dickinson's work has influenced many subsequent writers. Poet and novelist Marge Piercy says she found Dickinson an inspiration. "Like most young writers, I imitated a great deal in my early years. I began with those two parents of American poetry, Emily Dickinson and Walt Whitman. Everything truly American since is a descendant of theirs."[3]

LONGFELLOW'S *KAVANAGH*

We know from her numerous letters and from her poems themselves that Emily loved to read. One of the "hot" books of 1849 was a book by Henry Wadsworth Longfellow, entitled *Kavanagh*. This book and others such as Henry David Thoreau's *Walden, or Life in the Woods* or Emerson's essay "Self-Reliance" were part of the Transcendentalist movement, a philosophy that holds that individualism and idealism are more important than the material world. Dickinson's father would have disapproved of it.

In fact, *Kavanagh* was published to mixed reviews. "A work by Mr. Longfellow is always a matter of high interest in the literary world, while general expectation is still disappointed in relation to any enduring monument of Mr. Longfellow's genius,"[4] reported one journal (the reviewer's polite way of saying he did not think much of Mr. Longfellow's work). The story concerns life in a small New England town and Kavanagh, the main character, a young Jesuit who presides over the town's church. Remarked one critic, "*Kavanagh* is pleasant summer reading, but of a winter night one would ask a little more of the glow and fire of genius."[5]

Writer John Green provides an interesting critique of Dickinson's work on YouTube as part of his Crash Course in English Literature. Entitled "Before I got my eye put out," Green succinctly and entertainingly covers major themes in the poet's work. For example, he says that while it's true one can set all of Dickinson's lyrics to the Coca-Cola jingle "I'd like to buy the world a Coke," the more important quality of her work is that it has "a lot to say about the relationship between life and death, faith and doubt, and the power of individuals."[6]

Poet and Dickinson scholar Susan Howe says that Dickinson's work refuses to conform to literary traditions and that she is "clearly among the most innovative precursors of modernist poetry and prose."[7] Perhaps that is why so many authors still find inspiration in her work. Debut YA novelist Cindy L. Rodriguez uses the life of Emily Dickinson to inform her book *When Reason Breaks*. Set in modern times, the novel follows two high school girls who are seemingly opposites. Emily Delgado appears to be the typical good girl, quiet and conservative, while Elizabeth is Goth. Explosive and fascinated with death, she has no trouble expressing herself. What the two have in common is an English class where Emily Dickinson is the subject. And while Rodriguez writes that she hopes their story is "compelling regardless of the reader's knowledge of Dickinson," she also hopes that it will encourage teens to explore the poet's life and work.[8]

> **Transcendentalist movement**
>
> A philosophical and literary movement popular in New England between about 1836 and 1860. Its central precepts focus on the divinity of man and his relationship to nature.

Ralph Waldo Emerson was a popular writer in Dickinson's time, and one that she read and admired.

It is not just poets that feel Ms. Dickinson's influence. Aife Murray, a writer and artist, has been motivated by the words of Emily Dickinson to create visual works she calls Art of Service. "When I cannot express something in one language, I 'say' it in another. I learned to silkscreen in order to move language off the page and onto domestic implements—ironing boards, aprons, tables, chairs—and clothing. . . . My interest is to obscure the border between life and art, so that the viewer experiences the slippage-what is domesticity, what is art."[9]

There have been composers, such as Aaron Copeland and Samuel Barber, who set her poems to music and dancers such as Martha Graham who choreographed her words.

Dr. Lynn Margulis, a scientist at the University of Massachusetts at Amherst, has also been inspired by Dickinson. Her field of investigation is life itself and how it came to be. She has been known to use Dickinson's poetry in her talks to emphasize the wonders of nature.

As you can see, Emily Dickinson's influence runs long and wide. Perhaps poet Ruth Stone put it best when she said:

> When I read her poems, these original, hard as steel poems, and I feel the intensity in every word, words used in new ways, bent to her will, then I think she was self-sufficient, an artist whose mind was never asleep, whose concentration recreated, made fresh all that she saw and felt, as though she saw through the ordinary barriers, not as a visionary, but as a laser beam. But when I think of how little recognition she received in her lifetime, and how devastated she must have felt, though her fierce pride concealed it, then I am angry and sad. Yes, a great artist knows and can work in almost total isolation, but it is a terrible thing to have to do. The original mind seems eccentric, even crazy sometimes.

In her cryptic inventions, she broke the tiresome mold of American poetry. We still stand among those shards and splinters.[10]

Dickinson in the Digital Age

Emily Dickinson has a Facebook page. Maintained by Penguin Random House Publishers, the page contains all of the latest news on the poet. For example, as reported by *Daily Hampshire Gazette*, a movie about Emily Dickinson called *A Quiet Passion*, is currently being filmed.[11]

On the more humorous side, visual artist Rosanna Bruno is working on a comic book about Emily Dickinson. Some of her satirical work is online at *Bomb Magazine*.[12]

GoogleDocs Masters Edition allows you to enter text and get some comments and corrections from Emily Dickinson, along with other well-known authors such as Fyodor Dostoyevsky, Edgar Allen Poe, and William Shakespeare, though according to some users Dickinson rarely makes a comment.[13]

The Mystery of Dickinson

One might think when first reading Dickinson, "So what if we don't know the exact date she wrote a poem? Why worry over punctuation or where she placed words on the page?" But the issue of dating Dickinson's work becomes more significant when you try to place the poet in historical context—what did she know and when? Did she have an opinion on the Civil War and write about it or not? Was she just eccentric or did she suffer from a poorly understood mental disorder?

Though Dickinson left many poems and letters, she left mystery as well. And perhaps, this is one of the greatest appeals of Emily Dickinson: how little there is about her of which we can be absolutely certain.

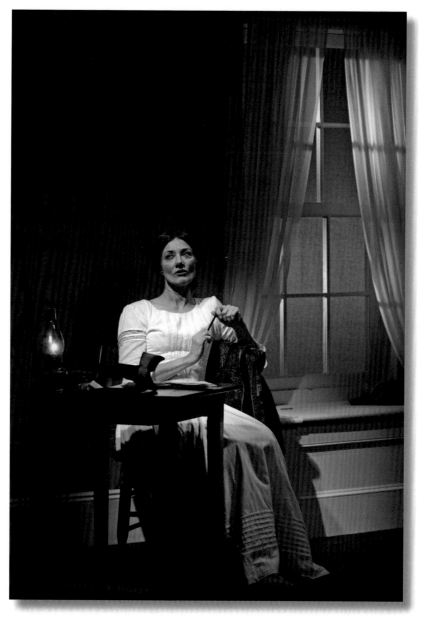

Today, the public remains fascinated by the life and work of Emily Dickinson. There have been a number of dramatic performances about the poet over the years, including this 2014 play, *The Belle of Amherst.*

For Further Study

The following two poems may shed some light on what Dickinson saw as the legacy of a writer and the value of literature, respectively. The first poem was composed by Dickinson shortly after the death of fellow poet Elizabeth Barrett Browning in 1861.

Her—"Last Poems"—
Poets—ended—
Silver—perished—with her Tongue—
Not on Record—bubbled other,
Flute—or Woman—
So divine—
Not unto its Summer—Morning
Robin—uttered Half the Tune—
Gushed too free for the Adoring—
From the Anglo-Florentine—
Late—the Praise—
'Tis dull—conferring
On a Head too High to Crown—
Diadem—or Ducal showing—
Be its Grave—sufficient sign—
Yet if we—no Poet's Kinsman—
Suffocate—with easy woe—
What, and if, Ourself a Bridegroom,
Put Her down—in Italy? (#312)

***

Unto my Books— so good to turn—
Far ends of tired days—
It half endears the Abstinence—
And Pain—is missed—in Praise—

As Flavors—cheer Retarded Guests
With Banquettings to be—
So Spices—stimulate the time
Till my small Library—

It may be Wilderness—without—
Far feet of failing Men—
But Holiday—excludes the night—
And it is bells—within—

I thank these Kinsmen of the Shelf—
Their Countenances Kid
Enamour—in Prospective—
And satisfy—obtained— (#604)

CHRONOLOGY

1830— Born on December 10 in Amherst, Massachusetts, at the Homestead.

1840— Family moves to a house on North Pleasant Street. Emily attends Amherst Academy.

1847— Attends Mount Holyoke Female Seminary. Meets Susan Gilbert. Also meets Ben Newton at her father's office.

1853— Ben Newton dies.

1854— Visits her father in Washington.

1855— The family moves back to the Homestead. On a visit to Philadelphia, Dickinson meets the Reverend Charles Wadsworth.

1856— Dickinson's brother Austin marries Susan Gilbert.

1861— The *Springfield Daily Republican* publishes "I taste a liquor never brewed" anonymously.

1862— April 15: The *Springfield Daily Republican* publishes "Safe in their Alabaster Chambers" and another of Dickinson's poems, again anonymously. She sends her first letter to T. W. Higginson and includes four poems.

1865— February 14: The *Springfield Daily Republican* publishes "A narrow Fellow in the Grass," inserting editorial changes with which Dickinson is displeased.

1870— Meets T. W. Higginson face to face in Amherst. Pens a few notes to his wife and later publishes these first impressions in *The Atlantic Monthly*, 1891.

1874— Edward Dickinson dies while in Boston.

1875— Emily Norcross Dickinson suffers a stroke.

1876— Encouraged by Helen Hunt Jackson to submit an anonymous poem to an anthology.

1878— Romance with Judge Otis Phillips Lord flowers. Samuel Bowles dies.

1882— Charles Wadsworth dies; Emily Norcross dies. Mabel Loomis Todd visits the Homestead but does not see Dickinson in person.

1886— May 13: Slips into unconsciousness at 10 a.m. Dr. Bigelow spends most of the day with her since she is suffering convulsions.

May 15: Emily Elizabeth Dickinson dies. The official diagnosis is Bright's Disease, a kidney ailment, but hypertension (high blood pressure) is more likely the cause.May 18: Obituary appears on the editorial page of the *Springfield Daily Republican*. Though not signed, it was composed by Susan Gilbert Dickinson.

May 19: Funeral is marked by T.W. Higginson reading aloud from Emily Brontë's "Last Lines." Maggie's brother, along with others, carries the casket out the back door, through the yard, and between the hedges to the graveyard.

1890— First volume of Dickinson's *Poems* is edited and published by Mabel Loomis Todd and T.W. Higginson. It is printed in Boston.

1924— *The Complete Poems of Emily Dickinson*, with an introduction by her niece, Martha Dickinson Bianchi is published.

1955— *The Poems of Emily Dickinson*, edited by Thomas Johnson, is published by Harvard University Press.

1974— Robert B. Sewall publishes a definitive biography, *The Life of Emily Dickinson*.

1998— R.W. Franklin, another respected editor of Emily Dickinson's work publishes *The Poems of Emily Dickinson*.

2010— *Lives like Loaded Guns* by Lyndall Gordon is published. One of Gordon's claims is that Emily Dickinson suffered epilepsy.

2013— Marta Werner and Jen Bervin publish *The Gorgeous Nothings,* the "first full-color facsimile publication of Emily Dickinson's manuscripts," [presenting] her words exactly as she wrote them.

CHAPTER NOTES

Chapter 1. A Poet Like No Other

1. Judith Farr, "Emily Dickinson," *Encyclopedia of American Poetry: The Nineteenth Century* (Chicago; London: Fitzroy Dearborn Publishers, 1998), http://gateway.proquest.com.ezp.lib.rochester.edu/openurl?ctx_ver=Z39.88-2003&xri:pqil:res_ver=0.2&res_id=xri:lion&rft_id=xri:lion:rec:ref:R00790142.

2. Ruth Own Jones, "Neighbor—and friend—and bridegroom: William Smith Clark as Emily Dickinson's master figure," *Emily Dickinson Journal* 11, no. 2, 2002, 64.

3. George Frisbie Whicher, *This Was a Poet* (New York: Charles Scribner's Sons, 1938), 28.

4. Richard B. Sewall, *The Life of Emily Dickinson* (Cambridge: Harvard University Press, 1974), 54.

5. Alfred Habbeger, *My Wars Are Laid Away in Books: The Life of Emily Dickinson* (New York: Random House, 2001), 172.

6. "Letters from Dickinson to Abiah Root," Letter 6, May 7, 1845, *Emily Dickinson Archive*, accessed May 27, 2015, http://archive.emilydickinson.org/correspondence/aroot/l6.html.

7. "Letters from Dickinson to Austin," Letter 16, October 21, 1847, *Dickinson Electronic Archives Online*, accessed May 27, 2015, http://archive.emilydickinson.org/correspondence/austin/l16.html .

8. "Emily Dickinson Photo; Between Hope and Belief," *Herald-Sun* (Durham, N.C.), October 26, 2000, A-12.

9. Thomas Johnson, *Emily Dickinson: An Interpretive Biography* (Cambridge, Mass.: Belknap Press, 1963), 29.

10. Dickinson 1958, prose fragment 80.

11. Richard B. Sewall, *The Life of Emily Dickinson* (Cambridge: Harvard University Press, 1974), 54.

12. Gary Lee Stonum, "Emily Dickinson in Context by Richards, Eliza (Review)" *The Emily Dickinson Journal*, no. 2, 2014, 105–107.

13. "Letters from Dickinson to Abiah Root," Letter 36, May 7 and 17, 1850, *Dickinson Electronic Archives Online*, accessed July 18, 2015, http://archive.emilydickinson.org/correspondence/aroot/l36.html.

14. Aife Murray, "Miss Margaret's Emily Dickinson," *Signs: Journal of Women in Culture and Society*, no. 24, 1999, 697–732

15. Ibid.

16. Ibid.

17. Emily Dickinson in Leah Bertaini Vozar Newman, *Emily Dickinson: "Virgin Recluse" and Rebel: 36 Poems, Their Backstories, Her Life* (Manchester Center, Vt.: Shires Press, 2013), 86.

18. Emily Dickinson, "The Single Hound," in *The Complete Poems of Emily Dickinson*, Martha Bianchi Dickinson, ed. (Boston: Little, Brown, 1924), 44.

19. "Letter J110 to Austin," March 27, 1853, *Dickinson Electronic Archives*, accessed May 27, 2015, http://archive.emilydickinson.org/correspondence/austin/l110.html.

20. "Letter J265 to Thomas Higginson," *Dickinson Electronic Archives*, accessed May 27, 2015, http://archive.emilydickinson.org/correspondence/higginson/l265.html.

21. "Letter L193 to Samuel Bowles," *Dickinson Electronic Archives*, accessed May 27, 2015, archive.emilydickinson.org/correspondence/bowles/l193.html.

22. Martha Dickinson Bianchi in Richard B. Sewall, *The Life of Emily Dickinson* (New York: Farrar, Strauss and Giroux, 1974), 650

23. Lea Bertaini Vozar Newman, *Emily Dickinson: "Virgin Recluse" and Rebel: 36 Poems, Their Backstories, Her Life* (Manchester Center, Vt.: Shires Press, 2013), 4–5.

24. Faith Barrett, Book Review, *Legacy* 30, no. 2, 2013.

Chapter 2. Reading Poetry

1. X. J. Kennedy, *An Introduction to Poetry*, (Glenview, Ill.: Scott, Foresman and Company, 1986), 1.

2. "Tips for reading Emily Dickinson's poetry," *Emily Dickinson Museum*, 2009, http://www.emilydickinsonmuseum.org/read_poem.

3. Jayne Relaford Brown, "Emily Dickinson Attends a Writing Workshop," *Visiting Emily: Poems Inspired by the Life and Work of Emily Dickinson*, ed. Sheila Coghill and Thom Tammaro (Iowa City: University of Iowa Press, 2000), 8.

4. Christanne Miller, "The Sound of Shifting Paradigms, or Hearing Dickinson in the Twenty-First Century," *A Historical Guide to Emily Dickinson*, ed. Vivian Pollak, (Cambridge: Oxford University Press, 2004), 203.

5. Charles R. Anderson, *Emily Dickinson's Poetry: Stairway of Surprise* (New York: Doubleday, 1966), 262.

6. Ibid.

7. Vivian Pollack, "Introduction," *A Historical Guide to Emily Dickinson*, ed. Vivian Pollak, (Cambridge: Oxford University Press, 2004), 5

8. Lori Lebow, "Emily Dickinson: 'She don't go nowhere', or a nineteenth-century recluse's guide to cross-culturalism," *Women's Writing* 8, no. 3, 449.

9. Philip F. Gura, "How I Met and Dated Miss Emily Dickinson: An Adventure on eBay," *A Cabinet of Curiosities*, accessed August 6, 2004, http://common-place.dreamhost.com//vol-04/no-02/gura/.

10. Sharon Cameron, *Choosing Not Choosing: Dickinson's Fascicles* (Chicago: University of Chicago Press, 1993), 4.

11. Lea Bertani Vozar Newman, *Emily Dickinson: "Virgin Recluse" and Rebel: 36 Poems, Their Backstories, Her Life.* (Manchester Center, Vt.: Shires Press, 2013), 50–51.

12. Joyce Carol Oates, *Readings on Emily Dickinson*, ed. Tamara Johnson (San Diego: Greenhaven Press, 1997), 27.

13. Michael Meyer, "Biography of Emily Dickinson (1830-1886)," *Thinking and Writing About Literature*, accessed July 14, 2015, http://www.vcu.edu/engweb/webtexts/ED303/emilybio.html.

14. Jen Bervin. "Studies in Scale," *The Gorgeous Nothings* (New York: Christine Burgin/New Directions Books, 2013), 9.

15. Ibid.

16. Ibid. 11.

17. Meyer.

18. Martha Nell Smith, "Because the Plunge from the Front Overturned Us: The Dickinson Electronic Archives Project," *Studies in the Literary Imagination* 32, no. 1, 1999, 133.

Chapter 3. A Funeral in My Brain

1. Joan Kirby, "Death and Immortality," *Emily Dickinson in Context*, ed. Eliza Richards (New York: Cambridge University Press, 2013), 161.

2. Helen Vendler, *Dickinson: Selected poems and commentaries* (Cambridge, MA: Harvard University Press, 2010), 64–65.

3 Ibid.

4. Caroline Rogue, "On 465 [I Heard a Fly Buzz], Caroline Rogue," *Modern American Poetry*, accessed July 14, 2015, http://www.english.uiuc.edu/maps/poets/a_f/dickinson /465.htm.

5. Ibid.

6. Charles R. Anderson, *Emily Dickinson's Poetry: Stairway of Surprise* (New York: Doubleday, 1966), 276.

7. Betsy Erkkila, "Dickinson and the Art of Politics," *A Historical Guide to Emily Dickinson*, ed. Vivian R. Pollak (New York: Oxford University Press, 2004), 153.

8. Anderson. 241–246.

9. Ibid., 243.

10. Ibid., 248.

11. Alfred Habegger, *My Wars Are Laid Away in Books: The Life of Emily Dickinson* (New York: Random House, 2001), 438.

12. Brent Kinser, *The Explicator* 58, Spring 2000, 143.

13. Ibid., 211.

14. Ibid., 47.

15. David T. Porter, *The Art of Emily Dickinson's Early Poetry* (Cambridge, Mass.: Harvard University Press, 1966), 46.

16. Frank, 213.

17. Cleneath Brooks and Robert Penn Warren, *Modern American Poetry*, accessed July 14, 2015, http://www. english.uiuc.edu/maps/poets/a_f/dickinson/341.htm.

18. Vivian R. Pollak, "A Brief Biography," *A Historical Guide to Emily Dickinson* (New York: Oxford University Press, 2004), 44.

19. Steven Winhusen, "Emily Dickinson and Schizotypy," *The Emily Dickinson Journal* 13, no. 1, 2004.

20. Brooks and Penn Warren.

21. Angela Sorby, "Education," *Emily Dickinson in Context*, ed. Eliza Richards, (New York: Cambridge University Press, 2013), 36–37.

22. Cotton Mather, quoted in Sorby, 36.

23. Vendler, 141.

Chapter 4. Divinest Sense

1. Lea Bertaini Vozar Newman: *Emily Dickinson: "Virgin Recluse" and Rebel: 36 Poems, Their Backstories, Her Life* (Manchester Center, Vt.: Shires Press, 2013), 118–123.

2. Cynthia Wolff, "Dickinson's Much Madness is Divinest Sense," *The Explicator* 36, no. 4 (Summer 1978): 3.

3. Ibid., 4.

4. Gary Lee Stonum, *The Dickinson Sublime*, (Madison: University of Wisconsin Press, 1990), http://www.english.uiuc.edu/maps/poets/a_f/dickinson/258.htm.

5. Suzanne Juhasz, *The Undiscovered Continent: Emily Dickinson and the Space of the Mind* (Bloomington: Indiana University Press, 1983), 20.

6. Martha Nell Smith. "Because the Plunge Overturned Us: The Dickinson Electronic Archives," *Studies in the Literary Imagination*, Vol. 32, No. 1, Spring 1999, p. 133.

7. *Merriam Webster's Online Dictionary*, 2002, http://www.m-w.com/cgi-bin/dictionary.

8. Stonum.

9. Elizabeth Arnold, "The Art of Poetry," *Research Frontiers at the University of Maryland*, March 3, 2003, http://www.umresearch.umd.edu/RFUM030103.html.

10. Cheryl Waker, "Dickinson in Context," *A Historical Guide to Emily Dickinson*, ed. Vivian Pollak, (New York: Oxford University Press, 2004), 180.

11. Vivian R. Pollak, "A Brief Biography," *A Historical Guide to Emily Dickinson* (New York: Oxford University Press, 2004), 16.

12. Helen Vendler, *Dickinson. Selected poems and commentaries* (Cambridge, Mass.: Harvard University Press, 2010), 188–189.

13. Lisa Melani, "Emily Dickinson—Nature," accessed July 23, 20014, http://academic.brooklyn.cuny.edu/english/melani/csb/liquor.html.

14. Betsy Erikka, "Dickinson and the Art of Politics," *A Historical Guide to Emily Dickinson*, ed. Vivian Pollak (New York: Oxford University Press, 2004), 172.

15. Melani.

Chapter 5. Walking With the Dog

1. Joan Kirkby, "Death and Immortality," *Emily Dickinson in Context*, ed. Eliza Richards, (New York: Cambridge University Press, 2013), 161.

2. Kirkby.

3. Marty Rhodes Figley, "'Brown Kisses' and 'Shaggy Feet': How Carlo Illuminates Dickinson for Children," *The Emily Dickinson Journal* 14, no. 2, 2005, 121.

4. Sara Levine, "Carlo," *The Who, the What, and the When: 65 Artists Illustrate the Secret Sidekicks of History*, eds. Jenny Volvovski, Julia Rothman, and Matt Lamothe (San Francisco: Chronicle Books, 2014). 78.

5. "Letters from Dickinson to Higginson," Letter 314, *Dickinson Electronic Archives Online* 1998, http://archive.emilydickinson.org/correspondence/higginson/l314.html.

6. W. D. Snodgrass, *De/Compositions: 101 Good Poems Gone Wrong* (St. Paul, Minn.: Graywolf Press, 2001), 81.

Chapter 6. Testing the Nation

1. Betsy Erkkila, "Dickinson and the Art of Politics," *A Historical Guide to Emily Dickinson*, ed. Vivian Pollak (New York: Oxford University Press, 2004), 158.
2. Faith Barrett, "Slavery and the Civil War," *Emily Dickinson in Context*, ed. Eliza Richards, (New York: Cambridge University Press, 2013), 206–215.
3. *Springfield Daily News*, April 10, 1861, 1.
4. Editorial, *Springfield Daily News*, April 13, 1861, 3.
5. Shira Wolosky, "Public and Private in Dickinson's War Poetry," *A Historical Guide to Emily Dickinson*, ed. Vivian Pollak (New York: Oxford University Press, 2004), 107.
6. Barrett, 212.
7. Ed Folsum, "Whitman Dickinson and the Fugitive Slave Law," *Walt Whitman, Emily Dickinson and the Civil War*, accessed June 22, 2015, http://www.classroomelectric.org/volume2/folsom/fugitive/index-dickinson.html.
8. Ibid.
9. Vivian Pollak, "Dickinson and the Poetics of Whiteness," *A Historical Guide to Emily Dickinson* (New York: Oxford University Press, 2004), 64.
10. Lawrence I. Berkove, "'A Slash of Blue!': An Unrecognized Emily Dickinson War Poem," *Emily Dickinson Journal* 10, no. 12, 2001, 1.
11. Ibid., 4.
12. Ibid.
13. Folsum.

Chapter 7. Letter to the World

1. Leah Bertaini Vozar Newman, *Emily Dickinson: "Virgin Recluse" and Rebel: 36 Poems, Their Backstories, Her Life* (Manchester Center, Vt.: Shires Press, 2013), 101.

2. Alfred Habbeger, *My Wars Are Laid Away in Books: The Life of Emily Dickinson* (New York: Random House, 2001), 457.

3. Marge Piercy, "Frequently Asked Questions," accessed June 30, 2015, http://margepiercy.com/faqs/.

4. *The U.S. Democratic Review* 24, no. 132, June 1849 (New York: J & H.G. Langley), 572.

5. *American Whitman Review* 10, no. 19, July 1849 (New York: Wiley and Putnam), 58.

6. John Green, "Before I had my eye put out," accessed June 28, 2015, https://www.youtube.com/watch?v=R4WwhOdk_Eg.

7. Susan Howe, *My Emily Dickinson*, accessed June 30, 2015, http://www.writing.upenn.edu/~afilreis/88/my-emily.html.

8. Cindy L. Rodriguez, *When Reason Breaks* (New York: Bloomsbury, 2015), 288.

9. Aife Murray, "Aife Murray: Artist's Statement," February 8, 1997, http://archive.emilydickinson.org/maher/statment.htm.

10. Ruth Stone, "Breaking the Tired Mold of American Poetry," accessed June 30, 2015, http://archive.emilydickinson.org/titanic/stone.html.

11. Scott Merzbach, "Filming planned in Amherst, Pelham for Emily Dickinson biopic 'A Quiet Passion' starring Cynthia Nixon, Keith Carradine," *GazetteNet.com*, June 10, 2015, http://www.gazettenet.com/home/17267572-95/filming-for-emily-dickinson-biopic-scheduled-in-amherst-pelham.

12. Rosanna Bruno, "The Slanted Life of Emily Dickinson," *Bomb Magazine*, no. 131, Spring 2015, http://bombmagazine.org/article/702033/the-slanted-life-of-emily-dickinson.

13. GoogleDocs Masters Edition, http://www.google.com/campaigns/ gonegoogle/masters-demo/index.html.

LITERARY TERMS

alliteration—Repetition of initial sounds at the beginnings of two or more words.

allusion—A passing reference, without explicit identification, to a literary or historical person, place, or event, or to another literary work or passage.

assonance—The repetition of vowel sounds within words or the rhyming of vowels rather than whole words. Rather than selecting two words that rhymed, Dickinson often used assonant rhyme in her poetry so she could use the most apt word choices.

concordance—Alphabetical list of all of the words in a book or in a set of works written by an author.

idealist poet—Poets like Emerson, subscribing to theory that "matter is a phenomenon, not a substance" because it lets them know "the distinction between soul and world" (From *Nature*, by Ralph Waldo Emerson).

imagery—The written description of a mind-picture appealing to the reader's senses.

meter (metre)—A measure of the rhythmic quantity of a poem, the way organized succession of groups of syllables are organized at basically regular intervals in a line of poetry, according to definite metrical patterns. In English this is by accented and unaccented syllables in the words.

metaphor—An implied comparison between two generally unlike things, usually referring to one object, attitude, or action as if it were another. An extended metaphor is one that is drawn out beyond the usual word or phrase.

naturalist movement—A theory in literature that emphasized scientific observation of life without idealizing it or avoiding the ugly. Compare with transcendentalism.

onomatopoeia—A word that imitates the sound it names.

personification—A metaphor that attributes human characteristics to inanimate objects, animals, or abstract ideas.

rhyme—The repetition of identical or similar sounds in unaccented syllables of words. An "eye" or "sight" rhyme is one in which words are similar in spelling but different in pronunciation, like "mow" and "how" or "height" and "weight." Dickinson frequently used sight rhyme.

rhythm—Recurrence of syllables at regular or expected intervals.

simile—A resemblance or comparison between two generally unlike things, usually introduced by "like" or "as."

stanza—A grouping of the verse-lines in a poem, often set off by a space in the printed text.

symbolism—A form of metaphor in which a person, place, thing, or quality stands for a more complex meaning.

Transcendentalist movement—A philosophical and literary movement popular in New England between about 1836 and 1860. Its central precepts focus on the divinity of man and his relationship to nature.

Selected Poems by Emily Dickinson

Listed Alphabetically By First Line

As far from pity as complaint
At least to pray is left, is left

Because I could not stop for Death
Bless God, he went as soldiers

Could mortal lip divine

Dare you see a soul at the white heat?
Death is a dialogue between
Death is like the insect
Death sets a thing significant
Doubt me, my dim companion!
Down Time's quaint stream
Dust is the only secret

Each life converges to some centre
Each that we lose takes part of us
Entreat us tenderly
Except the heaven had come so near
Except to heaven, she is nought

Faith is a fine invention
Far from love the Heavenly Father
Father, I bring thee not myself
For Death, or rather for the things 'twill buy
For each ecstatic instant
From all the jails the boys and girls
From cocoon forth a butterfly

Give little anguish
God gave a loaf to every bird
God made a little gentian
Going to heaven!
Good night! which put the candle out?

Had this one day not been
Have you got a brook in your little heart
He fumbles at your spirit
He touched me, so I live to know
Heaven is what I cannot reach!
Her "Last Poems"—
Her Grace is all she has
Hope is the thing with feathers
How happy is the little stone
How still the bells in steeples stand

I breathed enough to learn the trick
I can't tell you, but you feel it
I died for beauty, but was scarce
I dreaded that first robin so
I dwell in possibility
I felt a funeral in my brain
I fit for them
I gave myself to him
I had a guinea golden
I had no time to hate, because
I heard a fly buzz when I died
I hide myself within my flower
I know a place where summer strives
I know that he exists
I like to see it lap the miles
I lost a world the other day
I never hear the word "escape"
I never lost as much but twice
I noticed people disappeared
I see thee better in the dark
I send two Sunsets
I showed her heights she never saw
I sing to use the waiting

I taste a liquor never brewed
I took my power in my hand
I went to heaven
I wish I knew that woman's name
I'm ceded, I've stopped being theirs
I'm nobody! Who are you?
I'm wife; I've finished that
If pain for peace prepares
If recollecting were forgetting
If tolling bell I ask the cause
If what we could were what we would
Immortal is an ample word
Is Heaven a physician?
It's such a little thing to weep
It sounded as if the streets were running
It struck me every day
It was not death, for I stood up

Just lost when I was saved!
Just so, Jesus raps—He does not weary

Let down the bars, O Death!
Let me not mar that perfect dream
Like mighty footlights burned the red
Like trains of cars on tracks of plush
Love is anterior to life
Love reckons by itself alone

Much madness is divinest sense
My life closed twice before its close
My Life has stood—a Loaded Gun—
My river runs to thee
My worthiness is all my doubt

Nature is what we see

Nature rarer uses yellow
Nature, the gentlest mother
No matter where the Saints abide
No rack can torture me
Not in this world to see his face
Not knowing when the dawn will come
Not with a club the heart is broken

Of Death the sharpest function
Of so divine a loss
On such a night, or such a night
One need not be a chamber to be haunted
Our share of night to bear

Pain has an element of blank
Peril as a possession
Poor little heart!
Prayer is the little implement
Proud of my broken heart since thou didst break it

"Remember me," implored the Thief
Remembrance has a rear and front
Remorse is memory awake

Safe Despair it is that raves
Safe in their Alabaster Chambers
She died at play
She went as quiet as the dew
So proud she was to die
Some Days retired from the rest
Some keep the Sabbath going to church
Some things that fly there be
Speech is a symptom of affection
Split the lark and you'll find the music
Success is counted sweetest

Superfluous were the sun
Superiority to fate
Sweet is the swamp with its secrets

Talk with prudence to a beggar
Tell all the Truth but tell it slant—
That I did always love
That Love is all there is
The Bible is an antique volume
The brain is wider than the Sky
The butterfly's assumption-gown
The cricket sang
The daisy follows soft the sun
The Devil, had he fidelity
The difference between despair
The dying need but little, dear
The grass so little has to do
The healed Heart shows its shallow scar
The heart asks pleasure first
The Lamp burns sure—within
The last night that she lived
The long sigh of the Frog
The luxury to apprehend
The Moon upon her fluent route
The morns are meeker than they were
The murmur of a bee
The nearest dream recedes, unrealized
The night was wide, and furnished scant
The only ghost I ever saw
The past is such a curious creature
The Sea said "Come" to the Brook
The skies can't keep their secret!
The sky is low, the clouds are mean
The soul selects her own society

The soul should always stand ajar
The spider as an artist
The sun kept setting, setting still
The treason of an accent
The way I read a letter's this
The wind tapped like a tired man
There came a wind like a bugle
There is a shame of nobleness
There is a solitude of space
There is another Loneliness
There is no frigate like a book
There's a certain Slant of light
There's something quieter than sleep
They dropped like flakes, they dropped like stars
This is my letter to the world
This was in the white of the year
This world is not conclusion
Though I get home how late, how late!
Through the straight pass of suffering
Title divine is mine
To be alive is power
To fight aloud is very brave
To hang our head ostensibly
To lose thee, sweeter than to gain
To love thee, year by year
To my quick ear the leaves conferred
To tell the beauty would decrease
To the staunch Dust we safe commit thee
'Twas just this time last year I died
Two lengths has every day

Undue significance a starving man attaches
Unto my books so good to turn

153

Victory comes late

Wait till the majesty of Death
Water is taught by thirst
We outgrow love like other things
We should not mind so small a flower
We spy the Forests and the Hills
What mystery pervades a well!
When night is almost done
Where every bird is bold to go
While I was fearing it, it came
Wild nights! - Wild nights!
Will there really be a morning?
Witchcraft has not a pedigree
Within my reach!

You cannot put a fire out
You left me, sweet, two legacies
Your riches taught me poverty

Further Reading

Charyn, Jerome. *The Secret Life of Emily Dickinson*. New York: W.W. Norton, 2011.

Gordon, Lyndall. *Lives Like Loaded Guns: Emily Dickinson and Her Family's Feuds*. New York: Viking, 2011.

Johnson, Claudia Durst. *Death and Dying in the Poetry of Emily Dickinson*. San Diego: Greenhaven Press, 2012.

Liebling, Jerome, Christopher Benfey, Polly Longworth, and Barton St. Armand. *The Dickinsons of Amherst*. Hanover, NH: University Press of New England, 2001.

Newman, Lea Bertani Vozar. *Emily Dickinson: "Virgin Recluse" and Rebel: 36 Poems, Their Backstories, Her Life*. Manchester Center, VT: Shires Press, 2013.

Sewall, Richard B. *The Life of Emily Dickinson*. Cambridge, MA: Harvard University Press, 1994.

Websites

The Emily Dickinson Museum

www.emilydickinsonmuseum.org/

Official website of the Emily Dickinson Homestead, where the poet was born and raised. This site contains valuable information about online resources, printed materials and museum itself.

Emily Dickinson Archive

www.edickinson.org/

A scholarly website that provides a central place online for Dickinson's manuscripts, fascicles, and other resources that are "a starting point for the study of Dickinson's manuscripts."

Harvard Emily Dickinson Archive

hcl.harvard.edu/libraries/houghton/collections/modern/dickinson.cfm

Preserved by archivists at Harvard's Houghton Library, this collection contains over one thousand "autograph poems" and over three hundred letters.

Complete Poems of Emily Dickinson

www.americanpoems.com/poets/emilydickinson#poems

Provides biographical information as well as text of Dickinson's poems.

INDEX